creation. Strategy, growth, or attempts to increase the stock price without attention to Larreche's observations about this fact are limited or, worse, going down the wrong path.

Frank Cespedes, Harvard Business School, author of *Aligning Strategy and Sales* **and** *Sales Management That Works*

There has been a major shift in sales objectives from delivering revenues to the creation of corporate value. *Value Capture Selling* is the first book to embrace this shift, and I am thrilled that JC Larreche has written this modern and innovative guide to sales. I fully agree with this approach, and I am certain any sales pro will benefit by applying the valuable lessons within.

Philippe Chiappinelli, VP Sales & Partners Europe, Etiya

With *Value Capture Selling*, JC Larreche has created a powerful offer for readers. This book doesn't contain only theory, but it is also an interactive book that asks you to think, "What would I have done in this same situation?" By the end, you will be taken through a real sales negotiation experience, putting theory into practice and elevating your negotiation skills to the next level, where you will be ready to create incredible new success stories!

Enrico D'Aiuto, Senior Vice President Head of Global Sales & Marketing, Biotest AG

Value Capture Selling is a highly practical and forward-looking book that is a must-read for sales professionals and organizations worldwide. Larreche's book challenges traditional sales techniques and provides new approaches for achieving more with less.

Dr. Haisen Ding, Founder and CEO, World Executive Group and World Brand Lab

I am thrilled to endorse *Value Capture Selling,* a comprehensive and insightful guide that redefines the art of successful business relationships in today's competitive landscape. The book skillfully highlights the importance of commercial roles while providing a clear roadmap for creating value for customers and partners alike. It's an essential read for every sales professional looking to foster meaningful, collaborative partnerships—today and long into the future.

Dominique Ferrier, Global Accounts Director, FMCG co.

Larreche brings a wealth of expertise in sales and marketing to this insightful book. By focusing on the importance of value creation for both the customer and the corporation, this book revolutionizes the sales approach. *Value Capture Selling* offers profound insights and actionable advice that will equip you with the tools and strategies needed to drive sales growth, delight your clients, and thrive in the dynamic world of sales. This book is a must-read for anyone seeking to master the art of selling and create lasting customer relationships.

Dr. Marshall Goldsmith, Thinkers50 #1 Executive Coach and New York Times bestselling author of The Earned Life, Triggers, and What Got You Here Won't Get You There

Value Capture Selling shows how to navigate the ever-changing sales landscape with greater insight into the model of value selling that's traditionally focused on customer centricity. The author provides a novel approach that leads salespeople to a more effective negotiation position that satisfies customer needs while creating corporate value for your business. A must-read for anyone who wants to win more sales and achieve higher profits.

Gerhard Gschwandtner, Founder and Publisher, Selling Power

Selling with the emphasis on corporate value requires more business acumen and a stronger leadership attitude from sales professionals—that is, an upgrading of their function. In *Value Capture Selling*, JC Larreche provides sales professionals in every industry the knowledge they need to excel in this exciting new world. I highly recommend this book!

Omar Haddadeen, Inside Sales Analyst, BOMBARDIER

Larreche's timely book, *Value Capture Selling*, offers a profound, necessary understanding of the third sales transformation and related strategies to improve sales performance by focusing on corporate value creation. From leveraging the drivers of corporate-value creation to applying good value-capture tactics and closing, the reader receives a must-have roadmap and toolkit. I particularly appreciated the final section, Make Yourself Lucky, because if sales is a struggle for everyone, it is less so for those who understand it, and know how to enjoy, learn, perform, and be lucky as rightfully recognized by Larreche!

Joël Le Bon, Professor of Marketing & Sales, Johns Hopkins University, Carey Business School

This book provides the key for sales pros in any industry, anywhere in the world, to succeed by mastering the art and science of corporate value creation. It's an essential tool for sales success in today's fast-changing markets.

Mark Levy, The Big Sexy Idea Guy

Creating value for your company and your clients is the true definition of a win-win deal. However, many forget the corporate value part of that equation. *Value Capture Selling* helps focus your sellers not just on selling well, but on how to sell in ways that positively impact the health and growth of your organization. A must read!

Gráinne Maycock, Chief Revenue Officer, Acolad Group

Value Capture Selling is a great book containing many good answers for all executives seeing corporate value maximization as the next must-win-battle. This requires a total alignment around the strategy and accordingly, a full transformation of the organization, starting from sales.

Tolga Pekel, Group Vice President Corporate Strategy, Bekaert

This book provides sales professionals with powerful new tools to help them understand and implement value-capture selling, thereby ensuring that they contribute to the corporate value of their firm. A definite must-read for every sales professional!

Dominique Rouzies, Professor HEC Paris and Academic Dean, BMI Executive Institute

Value Capture Selling is an excellent reference for any sales professional who would like to improve their ability to create and capture value for their firm. I absolutely love the short but sweet chapter on leadership—it leaves a lasting impression! The ever-more-relevant concepts of BATNA and ZOPA are brilliantly demonstrated, and the emphasis on preparation is rightly hammered home! I especially loved following the story of Tom the sales pro—it felt like listening to a story of my colleague!

Manish Kumar Singh, Global Head of Marketing, Customer Services & Solutions, IGT Systems, Philips Healthcare

I recommend *Value Capture Selling* to any sales leader or professional who wishes to better understand how the science of sales has evolved in these increasingly complex and dynamic times, especially within the corporate environment. In this book, JC Larreche provides an insightful strategic perspective on the dichotomy between marketing and sales, while focusing on the essential skills and competencies needed by the new generation of sales professionals.

Giulia Stefani, Director of Global Sales Training & Education, SH&A, Medtronic plc

Just as Larreche's book, *The Momentum Effect,* inspired me to change my approach to doing business, his latest book—*Value Capture Selling*—offers a powerful approach to business and sales transformation. The book provides readers with an immensely practical view of how the work of sales pros is changing and what needs to be done to continue to be successful in today's fast- changing business environment.

Fabio Villanova, Sr. Director Commercial Europe, Thermo Fisher Scientific

Reading JC Larreche's latest book is like taking a walk with him and learning about a new universe that expands beyond the traditional definition of a 'salesperson.' It's a place where you will have an unlimited opportunity to innovate independently—regardless of what kind of business you are in. This is one book I will always keep on my desk!

Alessandra Vizza, Business Director EMEA, NSA & India, Corning Reactor Technologies

Professor JC Larreche has firmly captured the spirit of how today's selling model is shifting to corporate value creation. In today's digital e-commerce world, clients look to sales professionals to help them drive market share, profitability and client satisfaction when it comes to a more complex sale. As Revenue Enablement practitioners, it is upon us to ensure our programs are driven towards capturing value at the point of sale, which helps make our reps trusted advisors to our clients.

Russ Walker, SVP Revenue Enablement, Datasite

In *Value Capture Selling,* Larreche has given sales pros the keys to a more successful, influential and fulfilling occupation—this is truly a redefinition of the modern sales role. If sellers understand and follow the principles in this book, they will show greater leadership and confidence over their role in business performance. It's not an easy road. Doing Value Capture Selling effectively requires rethinking your depth of business acumen, the way you engage with customers and your market, and the emotional energy you bring to the job. Yet, it makes you as a sales pro an indispensable part of what must take place for the organization to create both short and long-term value.

Spencer Wixon, President and CEO, The Brooks Group

VALUE CAPTURE SELLING

VALUE CAPTURE SELLING

HOW TO WIN THE 3RD SALES TRANSFORMATION

JC LARRECHE

Registered Office(s)

John Wiley & Sons, Inc., 111 River Street, Hoboken, NJ 07030, USA

John Wiley & Sons Ltd, The Atrium, Southern Gate, Chichester, West Sussex, PO19 8SQ, UK

Editorial Office

The Atrium, Southern Gate, Chichester, West Sussex, PO19 8SQ, UK

For details of our global editorial offices, customer services, and more information about Wiley products visit us at www.wiley.com.

Wiley also publishes its books in a variety of electronic formats and by print-on- demand. Some content that appears in standard print versions of this book may not be available in other formats. Designations used by companies to distinguish their products are often claimed as trademarks. All brand names and product names used in this book are trade names, service marks, trademarks or registered trademarks of their respective owners. The publisher is not associated with any product or vendor mentioned in this book.

Library of Congress Cataloging-in-Publication Data is Available:

ISBN 9781394158584 (Hardback)
ISBN 9781394219858 (ePDF)
ISBN 9781394219841 (ePub)

Cover Design: Wiley
SKY10059426_110723

CONTENTS

PREFACE

I have a secret to confess to you. . .

It took me a *long* time to be genuinely interested in the world of sales.

Let me explain.

My early background was in computers—first, hardware and then software. I was able to write computer code in a dozen languages. But at some point, the field of marketing caught my eye, and I made the journey to Stanford University in California to do a doctorate in the School of Business. I didn't forget my first love, though, and I continued to pursue my interest in computer science there. I was fortunate to take several classes from John McCarthy, the father of artificial intelligence.

After these great years at Stanford, I started my career as a marketing professor at INSEAD, the renowned international business school in France, where I had earlier obtained an MBA. Not long after that, I was brought in as a consultant by marketing departments, executive committees, and CEOs at a number of multinational corporations.

One of the things I noticed during these engagements was that consistently, the first step taken by a newly appointed marketing director was to ask for a bigger budget. This was necessary "to be more effective," they would say. I wondered why the first reaction of these new marketing directors was not instead to try to be resourceful and find ways to do more with less.

I felt there had to be a better way.

Armed with my background in both computer science and marketing, and working with my friend and associate, Hubert Gatignon, I developed a learning simulator called MARKSTRAT (short for marketing strategy). With the MARKSTRAT simulator, I wanted to help students and professionals be more effective at creating value in competitive markets, while providing them with a risk-free platform to test their decisions on concepts such as product portfolios, market segmentation, and brand positioning.

The more I worked in the field of marketing, the more I was convinced that customer centricity was the best way to develop sustainable corporate performance. While I was certain this was the case, it was hard to prove because so many factors influence corporate performance. Short-term successes may be followed by long-term failures, or vice versa. I therefore decided to investigate the performance of the 1,000 largest firms quoted on the New York Stock Exchange over a 20-year period.

The key result of my research was a real eye-opener: the corporations that spent less on marketing (as a percentage of revenues) were the ones that achieved the highest level of corporate-value creation over this very long period. This sounded amazing to me, but it was the actual demonstration that "achieving more with less" was not just a vision but was being practised by some of the world's leading corporations—about 20 percent of the sample in my research.

Those organizations created more value because they did not need to push sales of their products and services so hard—they were already better targeted to their clients' real needs. And as a result, they enjoyed easier client acquisition, higher customer loyalty and retention, and stronger engagement, including word of mouth and unsolicited advocacy—leading to natural and inexpensive organic growth.

I called this phenomenon the *Momentum Effect*, and the book I wrote about it provided readers with a proven approach for developing sustainable corporate-value growth through customer centricity.

That was all well and good for marketing organizations, but how and why did I get so excited about sales?

Over all these years as an academic and consultant in the areas of marketing and strategy, I often met with sales managers and sales professionals. More specifically, I designed and delivered executive training programmes for multinational corporations in a variety of industries in North America, Europe, and Asia. These corporations included such household names as General Electric, Reckitt, Novartis, Exxon Chemicals, Oracle, Heineken, and many others.

During these training programmes, I was frequently astounded by the leadership qualities these sales executives possessed because they often far outweighed those of their marketing colleagues. No offence to any marketers out there who have other great qualities, but this observation tormented me until I developed a few insights over time.

My conclusion was this: the conversations that sales professionals had with their clients taught them vital and practical lessons about human psychology. And as they progressed up the corporate ladder—accepting greater managerial responsibilities—they were forced to further fine-tune their tenacity, insights, and leadership. Their skills were forged in a context where, in most cases, only the truly talented survive in the long term.

However, it also became apparent that despite their power and influence, sales pros had budgets that were generally much smaller than those of their marketing counterparts. Yet this lack of financial resources was in fact an advantage. It encouraged them to tap into their own inner resources, develop street smarts, and find new ways to reach their sales targets. Necessity is the mother of invention, as they say, and sales professionals are often forced to invent new ways to succeed with limited cash.

I loved having discussions with the top-of-the-top sales professionals—those individuals who collected armfuls of awards, enjoyed tremendous standards of living, thanks to their ample bonuses, hated having to fill out the admin forms, complained openly about bureaucracy and red tape, and loathed wasting their time watching management presentations.

What surprised me most was their consistent refusal to be promoted. But it all made sense when they explained it to me clearly from their perspective: "Why accept a reduced income and the pains of managing others in exchange for the stability and comfort of an office job?" These high achievers had strong personalities, and I was happy to observe how they could (most of the time) get away with their personal idiosyncrasies because management realized how valuable they were for the company.

I also enjoyed meeting the sales professionals who were willing to share with me their challenges and anxieties. At the top of the list was the financial uncertainty when the variable was an important component of the total outcome, linked to the need to make payments on a hefty mortgage and/or fund their children's education. Another frequent concern was a feeling that the task of selling was becoming more difficult over time—a steadily increasing number of demanding clients, more templates to fill out, greater acceleration of change, less internal support and cooperation, and less time to reflect and recharge.

I became fascinated by the world of sales because of these encounters where I could observe the everyday reality of the sales professional's life on the front line. It was in these discussions with sales pros who were, on the one side, facing clients, and, on the other, interacting with the internal resources of the company, that I could really observe the ultimate pains and gains of the level of customer centricity I had advocated for so long.

More recently, as I continued to interact with global corporations, I began to observe an interesting phenomenon emerging within them: the increasing recognition of sales as a strategic function. In some cases, this occurred when the heads of sales at some of the most progressive of these organizations were elevated to the executive committee, such as was the case at Hubspot, Microsoft, or Dell.

At the same time, the pressure increased in many firms to focus on the creation of *corporate value*. While the front end of the selling process, *customer-value creation*, will always remain crucial, this pressure gives more importance and urgency to *value-capture selling*, where the sales pros have to ensure that they contribute to the corporate value of their firm. This is the subject of this book and where I have built on my personal expertise in marketing and strategy to bring additional power to the existing skills of sales professionals.

Long story short, I am now much more than just interested in sales, I am a committed advocate. And I wrote this book to provide you, today's sales professional, with a new set of powerful tools to help you achieve even greater levels of personal success at value-capture selling, along with the success of your business.

JC Larreche

CHAPTER 1

THE ADVENT OF VALUE CAPTURE

I'll never forget my first meeting with Tom Werner.

Tom was a sales pro who worked for ELTRON, an electronics equipment firm selling to businesses in a variety of sectors. Before that, he had worked for a well-known manufacturer of soft drinks. He was 41 years old and an accomplished salesperson who had accumulated numerous sales awards and acquired and served hundreds of clients over the long course of his career in different industries. Tom had been with his current company for more than eight years—he was very loyal, and he loved his job and his clients. So much so that he repeatedly refused promotions to the position of district manager. He made a lot of money for his company, and he knew it.

Everything was perfect in Tom's world. That is, until he and the other sales pros in the organization were told by management that there was going to be a new emphasis on "corporate-value creation," and that the sales-incentive system would be changed to reflect this.

Tom had no financial skills whatsoever, and he was understandably anxious about the new emphasis on corporate-value creation and how this unknown factor might negatively affect his compensation. He and his wife Lola—a financial analyst for a major bank—had one kid in college and another two years away. Tom did not usually lack self-confidence. He knew that he had consistently been a top performer but wondered if he would be able to remain at the top and maintain his income, of which traditional sales incentives were an important component. Tom didn't know what he didn't know.

But Tom wasn't alone—other sales pros I have met wondered how they would be affected by their companies' shift to corporate-value creation. But not everyone saw it as a potential negative.

Maggie Murphy worked for the same soft drinks company that Tom used to work for—selling to key accounts and other retail outlets. At 32 years old, she was younger than Tom, and a college graduate with a degree in business. She chose a career in sales while many of her friends aspired to management positions. Maggie absolutely *loved* selling and the opportunity it provided to interact with a variety of clients in different organizations. She had done it for eight years and she was with her second employer.

The new CEO of Maggie's company announced a new strategy with top priorities on customer centricity and corporate-value creation. This new strategy involved a different emphasis in the sales process that the new CEO called *revenue management,* and which involved more attention to financial issues. While some of her colleagues found the changes difficult and threatening, Maggie enjoyed the opportunity to have new challenges in her work and to potentially benefit from her college studies.

Her husband, Mark, a computer engineer, whom she met at college, shared her enthusiasm. Maggie expected that she would be able to better demonstrate her capabilities in this new environment, providing a welcome boost to her career.

These two contrasting stories of Tom and Maggie illustrate what I call the *3rd sales transformation,* which stems from the increased emphasis companies place on corporate-value creation. This transformation is happening right now, globally, and it's beginning to separate the winners from the losers.

The sales function indeed faces major challenges that in many companies have already resulted—and will continue to result—in a reduction in the number of sales professionals and an upgrade of the role of those who win their way through. In 2011, *Selling Power* magazine predicted that by 2020, the number of salespeople in the United States would plummet from 18 million to less than 3 million. And while I'm sure many sales pros rolled their eyes when they heard of *Selling Power's* prediction, according to Statista, as of 2020, there were about 4.2 million employed salespeople in the United States.

So, what's going on here?

The most obvious and talked about challenge is digitalization of many sales tasks—replacing some and enhancing others. While most of today's largest corporations have been in a frenzy to digitally transform themselves, many of the changes made have not yet had a significant impact on their sales organizations. A study conducted by management consulting firm Roland Berger, in partnership with Google, revealed that, "although 60 percent of survey respondents are aware of the importance of a digital sales channel for their future business success, only 42 percent have a strategy in place to expand their digital footprint, while 33 percent don't even offer customers the option of ordering products online."

This situation must change, and sales professionals can expect their familiar role to be disrupted as organizations eventually race to catch up with the competition on the digitalization front. Many sales pros have already found themselves in this uncomfortable place.

But there have been other challenges for sales pros. The COVID-19 pandemic, which began its global spread in late 2019 and dramatically impacted the world for several years, led to differ-ent work models for both customers and sellers. The usual face-to-face meetings, lunches, and golf outings where sales pros built strong relationships with their customers were drastically reduced almost overnight, with Zoom and other virtual meetings taking their place. Businesses were closed, business systems disrupted, employees laid off, and incomes reduced or zeroed out altogether. Sales profession-als had to find new ways to communicate and build connections and trust with their customers. Some did and some didn't.

My aim in writing this book is to give you the ammunition you need to be not just a survivor in the aftermath of this 3rd sales trans-formation, but also a winner—upgrading your role in your company in the process. But what is this 3rd sales transformation? I'll give you the answer to that question after we take a brief look at how we got here in the first place.

SELLING AS PUSH

When management became a recognized profession—with business books filled with advice to managers, and business schools train-ing new generations of leaders—selling your products and services directly to prospective customers was described as the "push" element of marketing, while drawing prospective customers to your products and services through communications was described as the "pull" element of marketing.

At its most basic, the mission of sales is to convince a prospect to buy a product or service. This has always been true and will certainly always remain true. What has changed significantly over time is the sophistication of the approach used to reach that goal.

The initial emphasis of selling was naturally on describing the key advantages of a product. In a competitive situation, this meant emphasizing the different and superior features of one's product compared to alternatives. So, if you were a car manufacturer, you might create advertisements that tout your model's safety record, or if you leased copiers to businesses, your salespeople might emphasize the fact that your products go longer without breakdowns requiring service and leading to reduced efficiency.

Superior and differentiated features such as these were often described as the product's *competitive advantage* or as the product's *unique selling proposition* (USP), a concept originally invented in advertising. This USP was promoted by sales pros to show the superiority of the product and to obtain the sale without compromising the price. A price reduction was kept as the last resort to convince a hesitant buyer.

This approach was very effective then and is still practiced today, especially in situations of limited competition or when buyers are nonprofessional or naïve. In this approach, the objective of selling is to achieve a successful transaction, and the connection with a specific client comprises a succession of transactions. However, as the world became more competitive and professional buyers more sophisticated, new selling approaches started to be adopted by leading firms.

THE THREE SALES TRANSFORMATIONS

Over the last couple of decades, selling has thus progressively evolved as a more and more professional and glamorous function. In many corporations, the sales function has finally achieved the strategic status that it deserves and that it was long deprived of.

This advent of sales as a strategic function is a formidable evolution compared to the antiquated top-management view of sales as the lowest level of the commercial operation or the description of sales as the *push* element of marketing.

Sales has indeed benefited from numerous successive changes over the last decades, and with almost every company you walk into, you can hear about the different stages in the evolution of its sales function. After my own analysis of the way in which sales progressed to achieve its current strategic status in leading corporations, I have identified three major stages—what I call *sales transformations*—that have each had a major impact in upgrading the performance and the recognition of the sales function:

- **The 1st sales transformation:** Improving sales performance at the client interface
- **The 2nd sales transformation:** Improving sales performance through stronger cooperation with marketing
- **The 3rd sales transformation:** Improving sales performance by focusing on corporate-value creation

I describe these transformations in greater detail in Chapters 2 and 3, but let's take a quick look at what they are and how they contribute to the performance of the sales function.

- **The 1st sales transformation.** As competitive pressures in the global business environment increased in the 1980s and 1990s, there was a shift from seller power to buyer power. This shift forced a major change in how sales professionals approached selling. No longer could sales pros simply push their products and services directly to prospective customers—they had to make the effort to first understand the client's needs and insights and then respond to them.

The more advanced kinds of selling that came out of this 1st sales transformation included solution selling, relationship selling, and consultative selling. We'll discuss these in greater detail in Chapter 2.

Salespeople who embraced these new sales approaches at the sales-client interface gained numerous benefits, including increased performance, more-balanced seller-buyer relationships, more-stable win-win transactions, and much more. In addition, as more sales professionals were trained in these techniques, the job itself became more highly professionalized.

- **The 2nd sales transformation.** The focus of the 2nd sales transformation is *inside* the company, improving the interface between the marketing and sales organizations. The work these organizations do is complementary—when they're aligned in their goals and working together, they have the potential to dramatically improve business performance. However, in many organizations, marketing and sales are in conflict—their cultures are different, their priorities are different, their incentives are different, and they do not collaborate well.

   When sales and marketing organizations successfully complete the 2nd sales transformation, they are aligned in their goals and performance increases. Sales pros learn how to manage the interface with marketing to their advantage and to the advantage of the organization as a whole.

- **The 3rd sales transformation.** While both the 1st and 2nd sales transformations focus on the creation of *customer value*—the customer's perceived worth of a product or service—the 3rd sales transformation is the result of new business strategies that focus on the creation of *corporate value*. Creating corporate value clearly lies at the heart of any healthy organization. Creating corporate value in a business protects jobs, enables investment in everything from marketing and innovation to production and sales, and supports profitable growth.

The 1st sales transformation reinforced the relationship with clients and the 2nd sales transformation with marketing. The 3rd transformation concerns a new relationship and a new alignment of sales with *strategy*. It confers on sales a greater responsibility to contribute to the corporate-value generation of the firm. It also places sales in a unique central position between clients, marketing, and strategy, while upgrading the role of the sales function (Figure 1.1).

This new strategic emphasis on corporate-value creation implies a greater focus by sales on *capturing* a higher share of the customer

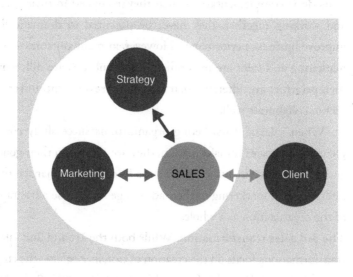

Figure 1.1   The central role of sales in corporate-value creation.

value created. This involves the enhancement of *value-capture selling*, which is the essence of the 3rd sales transformation and the subject of this book.

Value-capture selling is *not* a replacement for value-creation selling. In the first phase of selling, sales pros must demonstrate the value of an offer to their customers and prospects while gaining their interest. This is value-creation selling and it will always be crucial. As we will see in Chapter 2, the 1st and 2nd sales transformations improved the performance of this first selling phase by focusing on the creation of perceived customer value. In the second selling phase, sales pros have to reach agreement on the terms of the offer, most often with professional buyers who have been well trained in negotiation techniques. This is value-capture selling—when sales pros are given the mission to generate corporate value for their firms.

Do you believe that the term *value capture* is too aggressive? Would you prefer that your customers not know you are engaged in *value capture*?

It is fair that you ask yourself these questions. Sales pros have to build and maintain a strong, ongoing relationship with their customers, and this requires a soft approach. The emphasized, positive, and visible mission of sales pros in this relationship is the *creation of customer value*.

The reality on the other side of the fence is that professional buyers are trained in procurement techniques designed to capture a higher share of the value created by their suppliers. Suppliers and sales pros have emphasized customer-value creation for so long that they have been late to reinforce their value-capture capabilities to face stronger procurement tactics. It is thus time that sales professionals become more qualified in value-capture selling.

This obviously does not mean that the value-capture flag has to be raised every time you meet with customers! Customer-value creation must remain the objective of the first phase of selling. Only if there is customer-value creation can there be a sale, and value to be shared between buyer and seller. But in the second phase of selling, as on the procurement side, the sales focus must be on capturing a share of the value created.

To somewhat conceal this focus on value capture and appear less aggressive, some firms have adopted the term *revenue management*. This means that instead of just blindly focusing on maximizing revenues, one manages what *type* of revenue is created, especially within a wide range of products, to maximize profitability. This expression has been imported from the hospitality and airline sectors where continuous price adjustments based on data analytics aim to maximize the corporate value created.

Revenue management is a sophisticated form of value capture, usually associated with data analytics applications that give sales pros guidance on the optimal mix of products that provide the best profitability in a given situation. Revenue management software applications also provide valuable support to salespeople, helping them increase the corporate value obtained from a customer contract. But internally, it gives the impression that data analytics and management are sufficient to face the pressures of professional buyers, and it lacks the essence of value-capture selling.

The real challenge is for sales professionals to acquire the value-capture spirit and develop the new skills and behaviour that will increase their performance when negotiating with professional buyers trained at the same game. This is why I have decided to focus this book on the reality of value-capture selling, which goes beyond revenue management and is required to win in this 3rd sales transformation. It's taking the next step—making the shift from *bigger is better* to *richer is better*.

The 3rd sales transformation has resulted in new challenges and opportunities for sales management and organization of the sales force. This includes digital substitution and support, restructuring, updated evaluation criteria and incentive systems, specific additional training, and more. The 3rd sales transformation also has major implications for sales pros, including the upgrading of the sales function, richer information for action, broader perspective, more-complex objectives, more-sophisticated negotiations, and others.

The main focus of this book is on the *individual sales pro*, and what it takes to capture value and win in this 3rd sales transformation. I only mention the implications on sales management and organization of the sales force in passing—developing them fully would completely fill the pages of another book.[1]

HOP ON THE BUS OF CHANGE AND BECOME A VALUE-CAPTURE CHAMPION

It's clear that the world is changing and that corporations are a big part of that change. If your firm is already placing a new or reinforced strategic focus on the creation of corporate value, this will imply many changes throughout the organization.

For such a strategic realignment, it is likely that the chief executive officer (CEO) is personally driving the "bus of change." The most-innovative employees will quickly and enthusiastically jump aboard this bus to embrace and support the new initiatives. They'll get the best seats and might even have the opportunity to sit up front and help direct the driver.

Other team members might wait to see if the bus has any chance of succeeding before they get on board. Yet others will resist the initiative altogether and do their best to slow down the bus of change or simply refuse to board it.

In his classic business book, *Good to Great,* Jim Collins talks about the critical importance of getting the right people on the bus:

> The executives who ignited the transformations from good to great did not first figure out where to drive the bus and then get people to take it there. No, they first got the right people on the bus (and the wrong people off the bus) and then figured out where to drive it. They said, in essence, "Look, I don't really know where we should take this bus. But I know this much: If we get the right people on the bus, the right people in the right seats, and the wrong people off the bus, then we'll figure out how to take it someplace great."[2]

If the bus of change for focused corporate-value creation is already on the road in your firm, make sure you give yourself the means to get on board and to be a winner in this 3rd sales transformation—to take it someplace *great.* If your firm has not yet made this strategic shift, that's even better. Embrace the concept of *value-capture selling* and you will be ahead when it comes, or when you decide to join a firm that does reward this important capability.

THE FIRST STEP ON THE BUS OF CHANGE

Remember Tom, the super sales pro at the beginning of this chapter? You may recall how concerned and anxious he was when ELTRON, his electronics firm, announced that it would place a greater emphasis on corporate-value creation in the sales process. The idea was a new one to him, an unknown factor. And as we all know, change can be hard to accept—especially when you are anxious that it could have a direct negative impact on your personal bottom line.

As it turned out, Tom was not the only sales pro who was nervous about the new emphasis on corporate-value creation, and many of his colleagues expressed their concerns to management. So, to help them get through the transformation, Tom's firm organized a seminar on value-capture selling called the WAWS (We All Win Selling) programme. The name WAWS was selected to emphasize that the whole firm would benefit from the new corporate-value focus and value-capture selling.[3]

To their surprise, Tom and his colleagues actually enjoyed participating in the WAWS programme. Tom was relieved to finally understand the rationale for the transformation and its implications—especially as it affected his compensation. He was reassured and he appreciated the opportunity to expand the scope of his activities while doing what he enjoyed doing most: *selling*.

This book is based on Tom's experience in the WAWS programme and will give you the tools you need to be a winner in the 3rd sales transformation by focusing on value-capture selling.

THE STRUCTURE OF THE BOOK

Chapters 2–6 contain the fundamentals for value-capture selling as presented in the WAWS programme. Chapters 7–11 present the techniques of value-capture selling illustrated by Tom's first experience after the WAWS programme.

More specifically, in Chapter 2, we start by reviewing the key contributions of the 1st and 2nd sales transformations, emphasizing how the first phase of selling—focusing on the creation of a high perceived customer value—has benefited from new techniques and a better alignment with marketing. Chapter 3 explains the meaning of *corporate value* in more detail, why it has become so important in today's world of business, and how it gives greater importance to the second phase of selling, which focuses on value capture.

The new emphasis placed on the generation of corporate value enriches the role of sales professionals, and Chapters 4, 5, and 6 address the fundamental capabilities required for their enhanced value-capture mission: mastering multiple objectives, steering customer satisfaction, and developing a leadership attitude. Chapters 7, 8, 9, and 10 focus on the specific skills and techniques needed at the various stages of value-capture selling: preparation, strategy, tactics, and closure. Chapter 11 provides you with my parting advice—what you need to remain at the top: continuously learning to win and becoming a value-capture champion.

Finally, the brief Epilogue sets out the next steps you can take to gain the greatest benefit from this book, including my personal offer to freely practise your skills on the REVMANEX simulator.

If you are eager to get right into the value-capture-selling action without diving into the theory first, you can jump directly to Chapter 7 and circle back later to Chapters 2–6 to read the supporting concepts.

As Tom embarks on his first value-capture experience after the WAWS programme, you will discover how he uses his new tools—his *BATNA frontiers*, the *ZOPA*, the *RED and BLUE spaces*, the *closure map*, the *no-value* and the *no-deal zones*, and avoids falling off *the cliff*! And learn from his *shadow coach* what he could have done better.

Enjoy your learning journey with Tom and unleash your full value-capture selling potential!

CHAPTER 2

THE CREATION
OF CUSTOMER VALUE

The concepts in this chapter will obviously not be new to you if you are a sales pro who has already gone through the first two transformations focusing on the client and on marketing. But new or not, it is important that we establish a common understanding of the progress made in the sales world before we come to the most important current sales transformation—focused on corporate-value creation.

Walk into almost any supermarket, anywhere in the world, and chances are you'll find many different varieties of yogurts available to purchase. That should be no surprise since yogurt is a $155 billion global market that is expected to grow to more than $217 billion by 2027. Now, keep in mind that yogurt is a simple product—look at the list of ingredients and you're likely to see two main things: milk and the live bacterial cultures that are used to transform the milk into yogurt. Other ingredients are often added for taste and to improve shelf life—such things as sugar, fruit, spices, stabilizers, and so on—but at their heart, one yogurt is pretty much the same as any other.

So, what can a yogurt manufacturer do to differentiate their product from all the others and in the process attract more buyers? They can create the perception of value in prospective customers.

Yogurt is generally considered to be a healthy product—it is chock full of protein, calcium, and probiotics which have been found to improve gut health and perhaps even boost immunity (not a bad thing in these days of annual influenza epidemics and painful memories of COVID-19). However, Danone—known as Dannon in the US, the second largest yogurt manufacturer in the world—decided that manufacturing an even healthier kind of yogurt would create value for customers and drive sales.

Thus, Danone's Activia range of yogurts. Ultimately, Activia is pretty much like any other yogurt, with one exception: it contains a specific probiotic yogurt culture: *Bifidobacterium lactis*. Use of this particular probiotic culture allows Danone to promote the additional health benefits of its yogurt. According to the Danone Activia website: "Enjoying Activia twice a day for two weeks as part of a balanced diet and lifestyle may help reduce frequency of minor digestive discomfort, which includes bloating, gas, rumbling, and abdominal discomfort."

Do people buy Activia yogurt (as opposed to another, cheaper brand) because they don't care what kind of yogurt they eat? No, they buy it because they want to improve their gut health (and Activia promises to help do just that). And this is the essence of value-creation selling.

Chances are that value-creation selling is not a new concept for you. In fact, it should be very familiar because it is what all modern sales techniques are based on. In short, *customer-value selling* not only involves differentiating your product or service from those offered by your competitors, but also highlighting the benefits your specific product or service will deliver to customers. In the case of Activia yogurt, Danone differentiated its product from the many other brands in the supermarket by highlighting its specific benefits to consumers' gut health.

This focus on the *value* a product or service provides to customers, rather than on the product or service itself, is what value-selling techniques are all about. When you can sell your customers, either in a B2B or B2C setting, on the value your offering delivers, it becomes much easier to convince them to buy it.

FROM PRODUCT SELLING TO CUSTOMER VALUE

Selling is a very ancient activity which didn't evolve much at all until the sales profession focused on the creation of customer value. The traditional role of sales was very much to "push" products to customers. As I'm sure you're aware, this simply involved focusing on the differences between your product and a competitor's, that is, emphasizing your product's competitive advantage.

This selling approach sounds logical enough—it has prevailed for centuries, and it is still widely used today. It is the simplest form of selling that we can refer to as "trading." But it has its limitations in an increasingly competitive world. Picture the scene. . .

You recently joined a company that produces and sells filing cabinets to small and medium enterprises. There's nothing special about them, but your company competes by selling at a lower price than its competitors. Initially, this works well. You have achieved high sales volumes, and your filing cabinets are flying out of your warehouse. That is, until. . .

One of your competitors starts matching your price, erasing your competitive advantage. As a result, your firm is deciding between two options: (A) Further reduce the price and squeeze margins, or (B) Further reduce the price *and* decrease the cost of manufacturing the cabinets to maintain margins. Your company chooses the latter option and sources a different vendor to provide the locks for the cabinet drawers at half the price it was paying before. You lower your prices to your clients who respond well, and your competitor doesn't follow suit. It's all going well, until. . .

You start to receive customer complaints. Some of the locks don't work while others are sticky. In a couple of cases, the keys have broken off in the lock. Now you and your sales colleagues are facing unhappy customers. Your company is eating into its margins by sending out replacement products, arranging repairs, or providing full refunds. Meanwhile, your competitor—which stuck with slightly higher prices and higher-quality locks—is cleaning up.

This is product selling and not an uncommon scenario. Your company has not provided you with any clue as to the reasons why your customers are buying filing cabinets. Of course, because it's obvious! They buy filing cabinets to file things!

Dissatisfied with this situation, you join another firm which is manufacturing and selling ball bearings of various sizes that are used to facilitate rotation of wheels and other moving parts in bicycles, cars, kitchen cabinets, power tools, machinery, and many other applications.[1] On the first day of your new job, you are attending an onboarding programme where you are told, "Here we make ball bearings, but we sell value to customers." From the various presentations made in this programme, you remember a few examples of value offered to different customer groups:

- Smoothness of rotation
- Energy savings
- Reduced downtime
- Reduced TCO (total cost of ownership)

You were told that during the previous few years, the company—faced with increased competition—decided to investigate specific customer groups to better understand how ball bearings could help them succeed in their own operations. The company then progressively shifted its sales approach from focusing on product specs to focusing on customer value. This selling approach contributed to the company consolidating its client relationships and gaining competitive ground in several market segments. This new approach has now been generalized to the entire sales force and is the one taught to new recruits in the onboarding programme.

The contrast between the selling practices of these two companies, the first making filing cabinets and the second ball bearings, illustrates the progress made in sales on the client front.

Remember the Activia example from Danone? This product is not sold to end consumers as just another yogurt, nor even as a yogurt with a specific probiotic yogurt culture, *Bifidobacterium lactis*. It is sold for its value to consumers, a gut-health benefit. The probiotic culture is just mentioned to explain the reason for the consumer health benefit and give it credibility.

When it comes to selling Activia to the purchasing manager of the yogurt department in a retail chain—a B2B transaction—one must focus on the value to the retail chain, not only to the end consumer. There also, the probiotic yogurt culture is just a product feature. Selling to the purchasing manager will have to focus on the value Activia can represent to the retail chain, including higher margins, offering a broader service, or attracting a different breed of consumers to the stores.

Businesses that failed to evolve when customer-value selling emerged have struggled to grow, and in many cases, have shrunk or closed altogether. In the short term, they've seen their margins eroded by constantly having to lower prices or compromise on quality (or both!). However, it's over the medium to long term where the real damage is done.

Let's now see how this 1st sales transformation came about, what new sales techniques were developed, and investigate further the real meaning of *customer value*.

THE 1ST SALES TRANSFORMATION

The global business environment started to become more highly competitive in the 1980s and 1990s because of increased competitive pressure resulting from many forces in the business environment. Some of the most significant of these forces included the continued development of world trade and new communications technologies.

One key outcome of this increased competition was a shift in many sectors from seller power to buyer power, forcing a major change in the selling approach. Instead of just convincing the buyer to accept an offer on the buyer's terms, selling also had to make a greater effort to understand the client's requirements. This is when the client interface became the source of more strategic attention and selling improvements were made to develop a stronger client relationship, as opposed to just pushing products or services on them.

The *1st sales transformation* represents the necessary adaptation of selling to increased buyer power—a painful adjustment, but eventually leading to higher sales performance. Sales professionals accomplished this by discovering customer needs and insights and by making the move from just "product selling" to three successive, more-advanced kinds of selling:

- **Solution selling.** This first step in the new selling orientation is when you pay more attention to the client's requirements. The approach emerged from the realization that the main reason for customers to buy a specific product was to resolve a problem they had. So, the idea was not to focus on the product, but to instead focus on the solution to the buyer's problem. This gave sales professionals a broader view of the offer to be sold, which included the product, but also accessories and services. For example, a prospective client's warehouse forklifts might be old and unreliable, causing significant downtime. In this case, the sales professional could propose selling not only new forklifts to the client, but also maintenance contracts to ensure the forklifts are always in tip-top shape and to reduce unproductive downtime. A win-win resolution of a customer's problem.

- **Relationship selling.** As sales professionals turned more of their attention toward the client, this led to their recognizing the importance of repeat purchases and extended sales to the same customers in the future. With this longer-term perspective came the realization that the objective of a sale is not only a successful transaction but a satisfactory relationship with a specific customer and buyer. For example, instead of just selling a batch of personal computers to a client company and then moving on to the next prospect—ignoring the current client—the sales professional maintains and builds a long-term relationship with them. They do this by periodically checking in with clients, quickly resolving any product or service issues they may have, and offering solutions to new problems that may arise.

- **Consultative selling.** Solution selling was a recognition that effective selling in a competitive world had to start with the customer's needs. Relationship selling extended this to the customer's needs over a longer time horizon. It was natural that the next step to improve sales on the client performance frontier was to understand the needs of the customer more deeply. This consultative-selling approach involves asking questions, investigating, and helping customers identify and formulate the nature of their needs. For example, before recommending a particular product, a salesperson selling delivery vans to businesses asks the buyer a series of questions that help define the best solution. These questions might include finding out what kind of vans the buyer's company currently has in its fleet, what the company likes and dislikes about them, how they intend to use the new vans— for driving short distances and making lots of stops, driving long distances and making just a few stops, occasionally making delivery runs on unpaved roads—and so on. Only after gathering this information does the salesperson offer product suggestions that best fit the customer's needs.

From product selling to solution selling to relationship selling to consultative selling—these approaches have helped improve sales effectiveness through a better understanding of client motivations. This better understanding confers multiple benefits.

An immediate benefit is that salespeople who adopted these more highly evolved approaches increased their performance and gained an advantage over their competitors. This evolution also created more-balanced seller-buyer relationships, more-stable win-win transactions, and increased benefits for both parties. In the process, the sales approach has become more sophisticated—involving significant training of salespeople and resulting in a greater professionalization of the activity.

MODERN SELLING TECHNIQUES

It's probably no surprise that over the last couple of decades, many sales consulting firms, sales training companies, and book authors have worked to help sales professionals develop their skills at the client interface and continue to boost the client performance frontier. A variety of sales techniques have been offered—often with memorable names or acronyms—that combine solution, relationship, and consultative selling into proprietary processes. Are you familiar with any of these?

- SPIN selling (Situation, Problem, Implication, Need-payoff)[2]
- SNAP selling (keep it Simple, be iNvaluable, always Align, raise Priorities)[3]
- RAIN selling (Rapport, Aspirations and afflictions, Impact, New reality)[4]
- Challenger selling (challenge customers on what they are trying to accomplish)[5]
- Insight selling (gaining a deep understanding of customers and their motivations before proposing solutions)[6]
- Fanatical prospecting (a systematic approach to fill the pipeline)[7]

Most companies use one or several of these techniques or similar ones in their sales-training programmes. But if you analyze all these techniques, you will observe that there is one common thread that runs through all of them: they are designed to create the highest value perceived by the customer *before* the sale. This is the basis of all modern sales.

WHAT THE CUSTOMER REALLY VALUES

While it's easy to talk superficially about customer value, understanding its deep meaning requires a specific investigation. At its heart, *customer value* represents benefits versus costs. Economists often define value as the product features acquired for a certain price (value for money). However, that is a gross oversimplification of reality, reducing the customer to a "rational economic agent" and missing all the reality and richness of a customer's life.

Really understanding customer value requires going much deeper than simply features and price. You need to make a deep dive into the human elements of customers to discover how they develop an appreciation for value. Most often, you will need to explore the various components of perceived customer value that the customers themselves intuitively process but cannot articulate.

To guide your systematic explorations into perceived customer value, I recommend starting with customer costs. I break down these costs into four distinct categories, from the easiest to comprehend to the most difficult: functional, financial, intangible, and emotional.

Let's start with *functional costs*. This is when an offer does *not* have a feature desired by the customer, or when the feature offered is insufficient. This offer has a perceived functional deficiency, or cost, for the customer that would have to be compensated by a lower price, if curing the deficiency is at all possible.

For instance, I recently decided to replace my 4-year-old car. I really like my car, especially its style and comfort, and I expected to buy the 2023 model of the same type. But I wanted a plug-in hybrid that I could use as an electric car in the city and a gasoline-powered car when driving long distances. I made an appointment with Nina, the salesperson at the dealership where I bought my last three cars. I was very disappointed to learn from Nina that the manufacturer was not planning to offer a plug-in hybrid version of this model for a couple more years.

In a spirited attempt to cure the deficiency and make a sale, Nina offered to give me a deep discount on the gasoline-powered version of the car. But no discount could make up for something that this product did not have: the plug-in hybrid option that would provide the level of eco-responsibility I was looking for. So, despite my long-standing relationship with Nina, I went to another dealership to buy a completely different brand of car that offered the plug-in hybrid feature I wanted.

The next cost category is *financial*, which is not only a product's price, but includes such things as the seller's credit terms, delivery fees, the cost to maintain the product, cost of operations, and so forth. We are all most familiar with this dimension.

Intangible costs are things we cannot measure. Let's say, for example, that you've been buying a product from a particular vendor for many years. The vendor is extremely reliable, but a competitor's price is lower, and you're considering making the switch to the less-expensive source. However, there's some risk involved buying this product from a new source. Will they meet your schedules? Will the product quality be up to par? Do you trust what the salesperson is telling you? You can't really put a dollar value on this risk, it's intangible but it is nonetheless a real cost.

Then there is the *emotional cost*—an intangible cost that, when it becomes high enough, creates negative emotions for the customer. Imagine that you are a buyer in a company that has had a 10-year relationship with a supplier. Theo, the salesperson from the supplier has become a friend—you sometimes have lunch together or play tennis. A couple years ago, you explained to Theo that your company was going through a rough patch, so it would be good if he could drop the price a bit.

Your friend Theo responded that they, too, were going through difficult times, and although he would love to drop the price, he would not be able to. His boss would not accept a reduction, so no discount.

The following year, you asked again, and again you got the same response from Theo: "I would love to do it, but, frankly, we're still going through difficult times. So, I can't drop the price."

One day, your company hires a new buyer, Seb, from a competing firm—a company that bought the same product you did from the same supplier. When you compare notes with Seb, you realize that your friend Theo has been offering the same product to Seb's old company at a 10 percent lower price.

What happens? You get hurt, angry, mad—*emotional*. You might call Theo and demand to know why your competitor has been getting a discount, but you have not. And Theo might give you some excuse—the competitor's CEO and the vendor's CEO are golf buddies—then offer to match the discount given to your competitor, and even sweeten it with an additional 2 percent off. But you're hurt, and you turn down the offer even though the deal is financially better than what you wanted in the first place.

Your emotions tell you that you cannot trust Theo anymore, and so you then seek out a new vendor. It's no longer a matter of money, no longer a matter of getting the best deal for your company. It is about betrayal, a huge emotional cost.

Notice that from the functional cost down to the emotional, one goes from the familiar and visible to the deeper and hidden levels of the costs incurred by customers when they consider buying a product or service. And often, the deeper and hidden costs have a greater influence on customers' decisions.

Benefits track much the same way as costs. *Functional benefits* for customers could be anything from a faster microprocessor in a computer, to a bank that offers more-secure online payments, to a mobile phone with a better camera in it—and much more. If you need a particular function or feature in a product or service, and the item someone is trying to sell you has it, then that's a clear benefit to you, the customer.

Although *financial* is most often considered to be a cost, it can also be a benefit. For example, if you are planning a vacation and you need to fly to some far-off destination, the lower price you pay for a ticket offered by a low-cost airline—say, Ryanair, EasyJet, or Southwest—is a distinct benefit compared to the more expensive ticket offered by Lufthansa, Emirates, or Cathay Pacific.

An *intangible benefit* for a customer can be the prestige that certain high-end or highly desirable brands confer. For example, carrying the latest Apple iPhone, or wearing a pair of Nike Air Jordan basketball shoes or a Rolex watch. Or it can be the boost in morale employees experience when they successfully complete a rigorous, company-sponsored Agile software development training and can add the certification to their LinkedIn profile. There's clearly a benefit, but it can't be easily quantified.

Emotional benefits are also intangible ones that have reached a high level. It's the pride you feel when you drive down the street in your new car, the satisfaction you experience when you celebrate a special occasion with friends at the best restaurant in town, or the surge of happiness that courses through you when you imagine that the new outfit you're wearing makes you look 10 years younger.

As is the case for costs, from the functional benefit down to the emotional, one goes from the familiar and visible to the deeper and hidden levels of the benefits enjoyed by customers when buying a product or service. And often, the deeper and hidden benefits have a greater influence on customers' decisions.[8]

These four categories of customer costs and benefits create a rich universe of customer value (Figure 2.1), filtered by perceptions. Remember: the customer's *perception* is the customer's *reality*. What's real to them is what they perceive to be true, not necessarily what is true to you. As a sales professional, it's your job to make sure that you understand your customers' perceptions to shape an offer with the highest perceived customer value.

So, as you can see, to get to the heart of customer value, you must break out of the old, simplistic economic model of product versus price. If you remain stuck in that reductive model, it's going to be a tough battle with your competitors, and it's mostly going to be a battle of price—who has the lowest. In addition, you're going to miss a lot of important messages that your customer is sending to you—all the other factors which we went through. You're not in the customer-value world, you are in the simplistic rational economic world.

When you put yourself into the customer-value world, there's really no limit to exploration. You will never know the end of that world—the possibilities are endless. So, the intelligence of the salesperson, and the selling techniques they use, are all about exploring this unlimited universe. In the end, it's got to be the brain and the initiative of the salesperson to get this right. A good salesperson

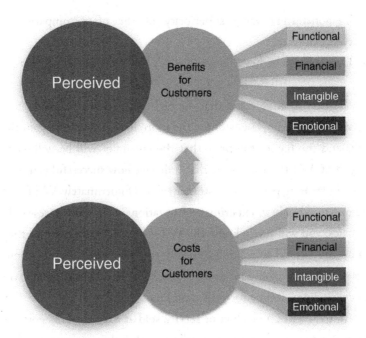

Figure 2.1 The customer-value universe.

won't blindly follow processes or techniques—they will think on their feet, be nimble, and adapt rapidly to respond to the needs of their customers.

As a sales professional, you must explore the rich value universe of your customers, searching for ways to increase their perceived benefits and decrease their perceived costs. Another way to express this is that you want to increase the perceived gains and decrease the perceived pains of your customers. In doing so, you focus on maximizing the perceived value for the customer. This has two specific purposes:

- Demonstrating value superiority of the offer compared to competitors
- Developing a higher *willingness to pay* (WTP) in the buyer's mind

It's easy to understand that the higher the value of a product or service perceived by a customer, the more likely you are to gain the sale, and the higher the price that the customer will be willing to pay for it. WTP is the metric that indicates how successful you have been in creating perceived customer value. Unfortunately, WTP can be measured only in experimental situations or in market research. In sales, you will rarely know the WTP of customers because they know they would be making a mistake in telling you the truth about how much they would be ready to pay. But you would certainly win in developing a feeling for your customer's WTP.

In the case of a product or service sold at a fixed, nonnegotiable price, if a customer buys it, you will know that this customer's WTP is higher than the announced price, and that they have made a good deal by buying it. In the more common case of negotiable prices, a customer's WTP is the highest price they would pay to buy a product or service. As we will see later in this book, value-capture selling depends on obtaining a higher share of the customer's WTP. And part of value-capture strategy requires anticipating the customer's WTP for different possible deals.

The 1st sales transformation has made selling a more professional activity, evolving from pushing products to focusing on the creation of value for the customer. At the same time, marketing evolved from the management of a mix of internal activities to a more customer-centric focus. This convergence offered new opportunities for an improved interface between sales and marketing, and another great source of potential improvement: the 2nd sales transformation.

THE 2ND SALES TRANSFORMATION

While the focus of the 1st sales transformation is *outside* the company—between sales professionals and clients—the focus of the 2nd sales transformation is *inside* the company: improving the interface between marketing and sales.

The effectiveness of the marketing/sales interface is most crucial for a high-performance organization. Both these functions are complementary in acquiring, serving, and retaining customers against competition. It is sales that concretely interacts with prospects and customers and brings revenues to the firm, so all marketing activities should contribute to sales effectiveness in one way or another. These activities include market research, market targeting, product positioning, branding, product information, traditional and digital communications, organization of traditional or online distribution channels, and more.

Using a warfare analogy, marketing is the air force and sales is the army. From a distant base, the marketing air force paves the way for an assault by gathering information, carrying out reconnaissance (research), and preparing the ground (generating awareness). But the marketing air force does not itself gain territory. That job is the province of the sales army, which progresses through the field with "boots on the ground" to gain and consolidate territory (market share). Both the marketing air force and the sales army are complementary and essential.

Can you imagine what would happen if the marketing air force didn't communicate effectively with the sales army? Or even worse, if conflicts arose between the two? The result would obviously be underperformance of the firm's sales effort in gaining and retaining customers.

While this analogy isn't perfect, the point is that both sales and marketing in your organization should be on the same side. They might do things differently and have different day-to-day priorities, but the end result they are both aiming for is the same: an increased number of profitable sales and a stronger, more competitive position in the marketplace. When you break it down into these simple terms, you can see that it really isn't rocket science!

And there is no doubt that this "odd couple" of sales and marketing has the potential to vastly improve the performance of any business today. Recent research found that 87 percent of sales and marketing leaders reported that collaboration between the two functions "enables critical business growth," while 85 percent reported that the alignment of sales and marketing offers "the largest opportunity for improving business performance today."[9]

While sales and marketing have similar objectives and should be aligned in every organization, the sales/marketing interface has traditionally been the source of conflicts. Indeed, according to the same research, 90 percent of sales and marketing professionals report that they are "misaligned across strategy, process, content, and culture." There are multiple reasons for this.

For one, sales is in direct contact with customers, and they sometimes have to cope with the copious customer grief generated by unrealistic promises from marketing, or from a lack of information or services. In addition, sales faces the requirements of specific customers—often in excruciating detail. Marketing is at the 50,000-foot level, working with information at the market level or customer segments—formulating market and product strategies based on analysis of current data and trends.

Because sales works directly with customers, they are naturally focused on responding in a timely fashion to their customers' requirements. Similarly, when marketing makes a request to sales, they expect a swift response. However, when sales makes a request to marketing, they often complain of not receiving appropriate and specific support.

To summarize, one could say that marketing and sales have two very different cultures, and in most organizations they do. However, this difference in cultures does not have to be a weak point for an organization. In fact, it is just this difference in cultures that makes sales and marketing each effective in the work they do. Any attempt to force one side to behave like the other would surely result in a drop in performance!

WHAT HAPPENS WHEN SALES AND MARKETING WORK TOGETHER?

IBM recognized the need for closer collaboration between its marketing and sales teams—so much so that it has integrated its sales and marketing channels into what it calls "channel enablement." The result, according to an article in *Harvard Business Review*, is a sales team that now focuses on creating product demand as much as fulfilling it, and a marketing team that can now link the amount it spends on its activities to the actual sales made, thereby proving the value of its work (and showing what could be improved).[10]

That's one brief example, but it makes the point. Marketers need to make just as much effort to understand sales as sales pros do to understand marketers! If you've long wanted to create more joined-up thinking in your organization, this will be music to your ears.

When sales and marketing teams start to work together within your organization, magic happens (no, really!). Sales teams can provide the consultative, one-to-one experience that they know works so well, supported by the marketing team's reach and budget.

This approach is one that more and more businesses are adopting, and it has led to a world where the customer receives a great deal of valuable, relevant, and focused information before any transaction takes place. Essentially, this approach makes the customer the centre of attention. In doing so, it increases the customer's WTP, so that they make buying decisions more readily having clearly seen the value of a purchase before committing to it.

When this happens, it makes your job as a sales pro much more enjoyable and productive. Marketing has prepared the ground, and by the time customers are in front of you, they are already familiar with the value of the solution you're offering. You can then focus on the most-crucial tasks of answering specific questions and objections to obtain successful closure.

THE MAIN CONTRIBUTION OF MARKETING TO SALES

As mentioned earlier, marketing is involved in many different activities, including such things as market research, market targeting, product positioning, branding, product information, traditional and digital communications, organization of traditional or online distribution channels, and so on. All these activities should, directly or indirectly, contribute to sales effectiveness.

While sales is in the heat of the action, marketing can spend more time and resources digging into specific market opportunities or barriers. While sales has to deliver short-term results, marketing can analyze longer-term effects and trends. And while sales focuses on specific customers, marketing can have a broader market and competitive perspective.

Sales and marketing are thus complementary and can help each other in many ways. But there are two specific activities through which I believe the contribution of marketing to sales is most fruitful: market segmentation and product positioning.

Market segmentation is the organization of a market into customer groups that have similar needs and characteristics. Sales pros well know that all clients are different—with different potential pains and gains—and that they should adapt to the client in front of them as opposed to sticking to some generic script or set of selling procedures. But segmentation analysis performed by marketing may alert salespeople to specific signals which can help them understand the requirements of a specific customer deeper and more quickly.

Table 2.1 is an example of market segmentation guidelines for sales, prepared by the marketing department of a company manufacturing electronic devices.

Table 2.1   Example of market segmentation guidelines for sales.

	Large enterprises	Medium-sized enterprises	Small enterprises
Contact	Multiple contacts including first engineering (prescriber), then department heads (users), last procurement (buyer)	Operations manager usually main contact, with occasional external advisor	CEO/owner is generally single decider and should be approached first to obtain other contacts
Relevant offer	Wide range of products and services	Low-medium range products	Lower-end products
Main requirement	Direct connection to procurement platform	Prompt delivery	Ease of ordering
Ordering	Multiyear contracts	Bulk orders	Single orders
Pricing	TCO (total cost of ownership)	Credit terms	Competitive pricing
Service	Resident service	Speed of service	Online service and ease of returns
Implementation	Joint co-development workshops	Onsite training	Online training programmes

This simplified illustration of actual market segmentation analyses highlights the differences between three groups of customers, based on field and online surveys. Of course, the separation into three groups is arbitrary—it could have been two, four, five, or more—and within each segment, every individual customer is different. But to be actionable and of any use to sales pros, market segmentation studies such as these must be precise and simple.

For example, Table 2.1 alerts the sales professionals prospecting large enterprises that multiple contacts will have to be established within the organization, and in a specific order that is usually most effective. The other elements also indicate that the sales pro will have to bring a broad range of services into the discussion. And for those sales pros prospecting small enterprises, Table 2.1 suggests that they should try to make a first contact with the owner/CEO to establish a trusting relationship. The other indications suggest that the sales pro should focus on a simple, basic offer in this segment.

Product positioning is another marketing activity which can effectively guide sales professionals. It represents the impactful formulation of an offer's customer value that should resonate best with the needs of a given market target. We all are aware of the slogans, old and new, of well-known brands that express their positioning: "The real thing" (Coke), "Just do it" (Nike), "Sheer driving pleasure" (BMW), "Think different" (Apple), "Helping millions grow better" (Hubspot), "Red Bull gives you wings" (Red Bull), "Don't be evil" (Google).

Product positioning is, however, more than a slogan. It is a statement to simplify understanding of an offer's value by customers. Product or service descriptions can indeed be very complex. Not only may some elements be irrelevant or confusing for targeted customers, but customers never have the time or attention to absorb all this information. This is particularly true in mass communication (broadcast, print, or digital advertising) where impact has to be achieved in just a few seconds.

It is thus normal that product positioning has been distilled into punchy slogans. But even in their personal communication, sales pros must concentrate on what is most important to customers. Product positioning can in this context be seen as the crystallization of customer value that we discussed earlier.

In the above example, the marketing department may propose the following product positioning for each market segment:

- **The privileged partner** for large enterprises: "We cover all your needs, including customized solutions, and guarantee long-term technical and economic performance."
- **The full-service solution** for medium enterprises: "We offer the solution you need, with full and responsive service."
- **The easy option** for small enterprises: "We make it simple, fast, and efficient so that you can concentrate on your business."

The combination of such market-segmentation studies and product-positioning statements should guide sales pros in their preparation before facing new prospects. Reciprocally, when sales pros provide feedback to marketing, this will allow them to refine their market knowledge and better understand the granularity of the market. This is really at the heart of an effective collaboration between sales and marketing, to the benefit of both functions and their firm's competitive performance.

POWERING UP SALES EFFECTIVENESS AT THE MARKETING INTERFACE

How can sales professionals win this 2nd sales transformation? By treating marketers as their "internal customers," high-performing sales pros skillfully use much the same techniques as they do for their prospects and clients. They know how to develop valuable internal relationships. They know how to identify what is most valuable for marketers in information or other needs, and to deliver it in the most effective way. In short, they have learned how to offer customer value at the marketing interface.

This ability demonstrated by some high-performing sales pros, however, is not shared by most—those who, as we mentioned earlier, find the interaction with marketing difficult, if not conflictual. The simple fact is that improving the performance of the sales/marketing interface is not part of most sales training programmes, and the average sales pro is lacking in this domain. To be fair, the same can be said of marketers. They too lack training in how best to manage their interface with sales as these issues are not part of most marketing training programmes.

While most companies have invested in extensive sales training programmes focused on customer value to win the 1st sales transformation, only a minority have undertaken significant actions to unleash the potential of an improved marketing/sales interface.

From my personal experience with sales pros who have participated in some of my marketing seminars, I can testify that the interactions they learned to develop with marketers were beneficial to both. Of course, it does not mean that salespeople need to learn every facet of the marketing profession, as they should focus on their main mission: *sales*. But they should be given the ammunition they need to interact effectively with their marketing colleagues so they can together improve their potential performance and their firm's competitive posture. As the issue is a single, internal relationship, this does not require as much investment in resources as does sales training for the client interface.

A first step is comprehension of the key elements of language used on the other side of the interface. This is easy and a priority as jargon is often the source of misunderstanding. Two other pillars of training programmes for facilitating the sales/marketing interface are, in my view, the market-segmentation and product-positioning statements mentioned earlier. A common understanding and alignment of sales and marketing on these two pillars are crucial for the firm's performance. A sales training programme—or, even better, a joint sales-marketing programme, focused on these dimensions—can achieve significant lasting outcomes to win the 2nd sales transformation in a surprisingly short time and with limited resources.

CUSTOMER CENTRICITY HELPS WIN THE 2ND SALES TRANSFORMATION

Some developments in corporate strategy should facilitate a better alignment at the marketing/sales interface. Most important is the generalized, increased focus on the external customer that many companies are adopting, not only in sales but throughout their organization. It started with a greater recognition that the traditional *inside-out* perspective—trying to impose the firm's products and approaches on customers—had many flaws that could prove to be very expensive in a competitive world. This led to a greater emphasis on an *outside-in* perspective, taking external requirements from the market and the environment to guide internal decisions.

The natural extension of this change in perspective has been an effort by many corporations to move toward a higher degree of *customer centricity*. In my book, *The Momentum Effect*,[11] I presented the results of a research project showing that companies that were more customer centric were able to develop exceptionally high, profitable growth with smaller relative marketing expenditures.

This finding has been confirmed in various forms since. For instance, a 2021 survey of 250 individuals across 180 B2B companies found that companies that reported a "very mature" level of customer centricity in the past five years experienced revenue growth 2.5 times higher than organizations that described their customer-centricity experience as "very immature."[12]

There is a great deal of research that shows the benefits of taking a customer-centric approach across your organization, both for your business and for your clients. Encouraging clients to make the best decision for them (which in some cases may mean not buying only from you), requires a significant shift in the way that organizations approach sales and the way in which they measure and talk about success and failure.

This greater focus on customer centricity is creating a customer awareness at the level of the corporation that existed previously only at the sales level! The concept of "value for the customer" that helped power up sales effectiveness at the client interface has progressively been adopted by many corporations as a central focus of strategy.

From corporate strategy, to marketing, sales, and other functions, an internal alignment has been developed in many companies around the concept of customer value, with the shared objective of creating customer engagement for the company's offers.

If you look at some of the biggest and most influential modern organizations in the world at the time of this writing (Google, Apple, Meta, Amazon, Airbnb, Tesla, and Uber, among many others), you will find they all have one thing in common: a strategy based around delivering incredible customer value and high levels of customer satisfaction.

Why has this approach served these businesses (and many others) so well? Because in making the customer the focus of their activities, these companies have built a strong base of engaged customers. They didn't start out by looking for ways to "monetize" their customers; instead, they started by delivering customer value and only looked at how they could monetize their customer base *after* they had achieved this (thereby making it much easier to convince people to use their services).

In established, incumbent corporations, this internal customer-centricity alignment has required, and still requires, an internal transformation involving changes in leadership, strategy, structure, and culture. But, despite the inherent challenges, the greater corporate emphasis on customer centricity and customer value facilitates the marketing/sales interface and offers opportunities for sales pros to make gains through better cooperation with marketing.

BUT THE CREATION OF CUSTOMER VALUE IS ONLY ONE SIDE OF THE STORY

The 1st sales transformation has helped sales develop as a profession by a stronger focus on the creation of customer value. This has been reinforced with a stronger cooperation with marketing in what we called the 2nd sales transformation. As a result, the first phase of the selling process which aims at gaining the interest of a customer or prospect for an offer has become highly professional. The recent progress made in artificial intelligence (AI) also offers new potential to help sales pros improve their performance in this first phase of the selling process.[13]

The creation of customer value alone, however, is not enough to thrive in the new world we are living in, nor to win in that new, 3rd sales transformation I talked about in Chapter 1. Focusing on customer value is undoubtedly important because it improves corporate performance and builds strong relationships between sellers and buyers. However, the question remains about how best to deliver value for the corporation while simultaneously delivering value for customers.

You have certainly noticed as a sales professional that you are increasingly dealing not only with technical buyers, who are on the hunt for high-value offers, but also with experienced procurement officers who are seeking the best financial deals for their businesses. Under pressure to make a sale, it can be easy to forget about what value the deal brings to *your* corporation, not just to your buyer's organization.

What we have now is a tug-of-war, with well-trained procurement officers on the side of the buyer, and sales professionals on the other. However, while the procurement teams know how best to grip the rope in this imaginary tug-of-war—and have a strategy that allows them to work together to powerfully capture value— sales professionals, for the most part, are still missing some important knowledge. They aren't always pulling in the same direction, and they may not have quite as good a grip on the rope.

This is where the 3rd sales transformation for corporate-value creation comes into play—the topic of Chapter 3.

CHAPTER 3

THE CREATION OF CORPORATE VALUE

While the 1st sales transformation to higher selling performance focuses on discovering customer needs and insights, and the 2nd sales transformation focuses on aligning the purpose of the marketing and sales functions within organizations—both resulting in the creation of *customer* value—the 3rd sales transformation focuses on the creation of *corporate* value.

But what exactly is the difference between customer value and corporate value, and why should we care?

Defined in simple terms, *customer value* is the customer's perceived worth of a product or service. If, for example, the product is an automobile, customers place value on such things as reliability, cost, style, comfort, fuel efficiency, and more. Similarly, when purchasing a ride-sharing service such as Uber, customers place value on many of the same attributes, including reliability, cost, style, comfort, and other factors. When making a buying decision, customers balance the cost of a product or service versus the benefits they expect to receive from it.

Corporate value, on the other hand, is something quite different. It is the current worth of a business—that is, how much someone would be willing to pay for it, or more commonly, for a share of it—and it is a direct reflection of the business's strength and the performance of its management team.

Corporate value is indeed the single most important measure of the strength of a business as it influences:

- Its worth to shareholders, banks, and financial partners—current and prospective
- Its attractiveness to current and future employees, customers, and commercial partners
- Its ability to make strategic investments in innovation, capacity, geographic expansion, and other areas
- Its power relative to competition

Assessing this corporate value will be based on the returns (profits or cashflows) that the business is expected to provide in the future. Consider this simple example: If you own a restaurant (excluding the real estate that you rent), its value depends on its current profitability, but even more on its expected future returns. This will have to be estimated based on a variety of variables, including your ability to attract new customers and the evolution of competition. A potential buyer for your restaurant would look at these different variables to estimate future returns and propose to you a price corresponding to its assessed value.

In the financial world, the value of a business is estimated by financial analysts who amalgamate all the information they can obtain to project the business's expected future returns. They then use sophisticated tools (e.g., discounted cash flows, taking into account the cost of capital and other considerations) to come up with an estimated value of the business. For a company listed on a stock exchange, its corporate value is equal to its market capitalization, that is, the share price multiplied by the number of shares issued by the company. For instance, one of the most valuable companies in the world is Apple and its market capitalization was $2.4 trillion in February 2023.

The value of a business will evolve continuously depending on a large number of factors, including many not under the control of management, such as changes in the economic, political, social, or competitive environment. The objective of management, however, is to increase the strength of the business and its value, despite all the uncertainties due to these environmental changes. This is the quintessence of the overall mission of management.

For a long time, it has been implicitly assumed in corporate boardrooms that revenue growth would automatically increase the strength and the value of a business, that is, *bigger is better*. At the turn of the century, this implicit assumption proved to be wrong as it led in many cases to value *destruction* instead of value *creation*.

As a result, many corporations refocused on actual value creation rather than its simplistic substitute, revenue growth. Cascading down the corporate organization, this sparked the 3rd sales transformation and the shift from the *bigger is better* mindset to the new, *richer is better* mindset. But before we dig deeper into this 3rd sales transformation, let's first make sure we appreciate the significance of this refocus by looking at one of the most dramatic shifts from revenue growth to corporate-value creation ever: General Electric Company (GE).

GENERAL ELECTRIC'S BIG SHIFT

In 1981, Jack Welch was named GE's chairman and CEO—the youngest chief executive in this company's long and fabled history. His focus was on growing revenue by making an already sprawling, global conglomerate bigger. Bigger was better, and bigger meant being number one.

To accomplish this, Welch introduced a ruthless cost-cutting programme to generate cash and give himself the means to embark on hundreds of acquisitions, such as the $6.4 billion purchase of RCA—which included the NBC television network—in a bid to expand GE's reach and influence. More than $25 billion was spent on these acquisitions during Welch's tenure, shifting GE's emphasis from manufacturing into financial services and other business areas while substantially increasing foreign sales.

In the short term, Welch's approach dramatically increased GE's corporate value—in 1993, the company was named the most valuable company on the US stock market. The company's revenue grew from $27 billion to $126 billion—and its market cap ballooned from about $14 billion to close to $400 billion—between the time Welch became GE's chief executive and when he retired in 2001. *The Financial Times* named GE the "world's most respected company," and *Fortune* bestowed Welch with the title, "manager of the century." However, bigger didn't mean better forever.

When Jeffrey Immelt took over from Welch in 2001, he initially continued his predecessor's approach to doing business—spending $9 billion on acquisitions during his first year as CEO. But the company faced major economic headwinds (see Table 3.1). The 9/11 attacks battered GE's insurance and jet engine businesses, and the 2008 global financial crisis hit the company's financial businesses

Table 3.1   General Electric: revenues vs corporate value ($ billions).

	1981	2001	2008	2017	2021
Annual revenues	27	126	183	120	74
Market cap at 12/31	14	398	161	151	104

particularly hard. Immelt eventually decided that bigger wasn't necessarily better.

After years of revenue-led growth, Immelt made GE smaller by exiting a variety of different businesses, including appliances, plastics, television (NBCUniversal), financial services, and its light bulb business. All told, GE sold off 370 assets while Immelt was in charge. And while the company's annual revenue peaked under his watch, at $183 billion in 2008, by the time he stepped down in 2017, annual revenues had shrunk to $120 billion. This downward spiral continued after Immelt left GE. Total revenue for 2021 was just $74 billion. Overall, in the 20 years after Jack Welch, from 2001 to 2021, revenues dropped by 41 percent and market capitalization by 74 percent.

That same year, chairman and CEO H. Lawrence Culp—the first CEO to be brought in from outside the company—announced that GE would be shrunk further by splitting it into three smaller businesses focused on aviation, healthcare, and energy. This dismantling of GE would officially complete the 20-year shift from a strategy of revenue growth to one of corporate-value creation.

As Culp was quoted in a GE press release, "By creating three industry-leading, global, public companies, each can benefit from *greater focus, tailored capital allocation, and strategic flexibility to drive long-term growth and value for customers, investors, and employees*" [emphasis mine]. These carefully crafted words clearly express the new requirements of corporations to create customer *and* corporate value.[1]

This is, of course, easier said than done. For GE, these three separate businesses will have to create value systematically, and their sales forces will need to play a major role in this—it can't just be driven from the top.

THE SOURCES OF VALUE DESTRUCTION

Jack Welch's focus on revenue growth through cost cutting and acquisitions was not sustainable over the long run. Why not?

The thing is, in the 1980s and 1990s, when GE was led by Jack Welch, business was operating in a relatively favourable global environment, with sustained growth. Revenue growth by and large resulted in value growth. At that time, business leaders widely believed that an increase in revenues would automatically lead to an increase in corporate value due to competitive power, economies of scale, and other forces. In fact, Jack Welch was determined that GE would be ranked either first or second in every business they were in. If a business unit couldn't meet that standard, then it was sold off.

And this strategy worked—until it didn't. Focusing on revenue growth, hoping that it will lead to corporate-value growth, used to be a reliably successful approach. It isn't anymore.

At the turn of the century, we entered a much more tumultuous and competitive VUCA[2] (volatile, uncertain, complex, and ambiguous) business environment, which has been a *stress test* for corporate value: businesses that had grown in size in an incoherent way started to be shaken, and the illusion of value creation collapsed, leading to value destruction. And this stress test got only tougher as the business environment later became even more VUCA with pandemics and geopolitical instability.

While the VUCA world is testing the capacity of businesses to create value, the seeds of value destruction are already present in their efforts to generate revenue growth.

When an organization's primary focus is to increase revenue, salespeople will be incentivized to go to any lengths to achieve that goal. This often means offering discounts or price cuts. However, while this might get the business one more customer, it erodes their margins. In the short term, decreasing margins is one of the most direct ways in which revenues can grow while corporate value is destroyed.

When businesses become so desperate for sales that they offer discounts, and customers let others know about it, this sets a bad precedent for the businesses that offered the discounts. Not only will the customers who bought at a discount be unwilling to pay full price for services or products in the future, but other customers will want the same (or an even better!) deal.

At this point, the business is stuck between a rock and a hard place. If it gives in, margins are eroded, and corporate value is destroyed. However, if the business refuses to continue to offer the discounts to its customers, they will be motivated to seek other suppliers, destroying corporate value. Once a company falls into this downward spiral of value destruction, it is very hard to clamber out.

The other factor to consider in the short-term picture is the increasing costs the business faces. If a company aggressively expands or makes acquisitions to become bigger, a steady stream of money must be invested to maintain that growth. But if these investments do not generate sustainable returns in the future, or if a company simply fails to make these ongoing investments, this too may destroy corporate value despite the short-term revenue growth.

While both of these actions have a direct and negative effect on value creation, they are not the most insidious or dangerous factors when it comes to value destruction. The factors every organization needs to be on the alert for are those that have an impact in the medium to long term.

Remember the example I shared in Chapter 2 about the fictional filing cabinet company? This is a very simplistic example, but it does illustrate well the three main ways in which a business's value can be destroyed from the short to the medium and long term.

The first, immediate way is a *decline in profitability* due to price cuts or discounts that reduce margins.

The second way, in the medium term, is *loss of market share* which can occur for two reasons. Either a company increases its prices and accepts a lower sales volume as a result, or it delivers a poor customer experience and people abandon the business. In both these scenarios, the outcome is a smaller portion of the market.

A *drop in customer satisfaction* is the third way in which a company's value can be destroyed, usually in the long term. Not only will this result in a loss of market share as customers leave a company in favour of its competitors, but it can also result in poor reviews and reputational damage that cause prospective customers—and employees and partners—to avoid the business altogether and seek out other alternatives. In addition, it is extremely difficult to recover from poor reviews and reputational damage, extending the organizational pain over a longer period of time.

CHANGING THE YARDSTICK FOR CORPORATE SUCCESS

As you can see, bigger doesn't necessarily mean better—at least in terms of revenues. The companies that are in the best position to thrive now and in the future are the ones that have changed the yard-stick by which they measure their success to a new one: *corporate-value creation.* Consider the example of Tesla versus General Motors.

Tesla's revenue in 2021 was around $54 billion, while GM's (General Motors) revenue was more than double that amount at $127 billion. However, Tesla's market cap at the end of 2021 was just over $1 trillion, while General Motors was a fraction of that at $85 billion. This means that with revenues less than half GM's, Tesla had a corporate value more than 12 times GM's! Furthermore, Tables 3.2 and 3.3 illustrate well the distinction between short-term revenues and corporate value which is based on an anticipation of future performance.

Table 3.2 Tesla vs GM: revenues ($ billions).

Year	Tesla	GM
2021	54	127
2022	81	157

In 2022, Tesla experienced a number of major problems, includ-ing rising materials costs, shortages, employee quarantines and plant shutdowns in China, and increasing competition. Its revenues still grew by 50 percent in 2022 but its market capitalization dropped below $400 billion during the final weeks of 2022. However, it

Table 3.3 Tesla vs GM : market capitalization ($ billions).

Date	Tesla	GM
December 31, 2021	1,064	85
December 31, 2022	389	48
March 31, 2023	656	51

recovered to more than $650 billion by March 2023. While this instability appears to be dramatic, Tesla's market capitalization is still colossal relative to its revenue. And despite the adverse events of 2022, it is more than 12 times GM's market capitalization, a similar ratio as at the end of 2021.This clearly indicates that, despite the challenges encountered in 2022, financial analysts still believe that Tesla has a strong capability to generate profits in the long term.

There are similar patterns with Amazon versus Walmart, Hubspot versus IBM, and others where younger, more-agile companies born in the new economy have higher corporate values with less revenues than their legacy competitors. And, also, a stronger resilience when facing challenges. These cases, and many others like them, prove that bigger isn't better—*richer* is better.

Why is this the case? Corporations born in the new economy have been designed from the start with customer centricity, marketing-sales integration, and corporate-value creation as part of their DNA and do not need to go through these transformations. They are thus ahead of older, established corporations. But they are not immune to arrogance and complacency, which can lead to a regression in their performance. They should indeed be careful not to lose sight of their DNA.

It's clear that many companies have not yet changed their yardstick for measuring success from revenues to corporate-value creation. Some of them have not yet gone through the 1st or 2nd sales transformations, much less the 3rd, as they are still enjoying favourable times because of specific situations (monopolies, weak competition, unique offer, high switching costs for customers, and so on). Under the increasing pressures of global competition or of other environmental forces, some corporations will find themselves in a difficult situation when they are forced to simultaneously go through multiple sales transformations as they embrace corporate-value creation.

Firms that have neglected corporate value can be the target of investors who have detected their underexploited potential. These investors are known as *shareholder activists*—shareholders who use their equity stake to bring change within the company. They include individual shareholders, private equity firms and funds, and more. Some private equity investors (dubbed "corporate raiders") found they could make a significant profit by acquiring companies against their will through hostile takeovers, stripping out the assets and then leaving them severely weakened—often on the edge of bankruptcy. This is the aggressive way to capture corporate value!

When taking total control of a company, or only an influential position, shareholder activists focus on a clear objective: selling their acquired shares after a few years and making a substantial gain due to the realization of an unexploited potential. For instance, RJR Nabisco, Hilton Hotels Corporation, and more recently, Disney and Pernod Ricard were all the subject of such investments by KKR, Blackstone, Vanguard, Blackrock, and Elliott.

When corporate leaders fear their company might be the target of shareholder activists—losing control of their business—they often shift their focus to corporate-value creation.

Shareholders, large and small, all want to see the same outcome in a business: corporate-value creation. They themselves need funds to finance their own investments or pay for their retirement, and it makes perfect sense that they prefer companies that place their focus there. Activist investors have played a major role in forcing corporations to transform themselves, using the threat of firing the current executive management team and replacing it with a team that has its priorities straight—the creation of corporate value.

Business Transformation for Corporate-Value Creation

The idea of creating corporate value is not a new one, nor is it particularly novel. Companies have long sought out ways to create corporate value. However, what *is* new is the increased external pressure put on corporate leaders to make the creation of corporate value the central mission of a corporation. Also new is the growing realization that this is not only good for shareholders, but that it is essential for the sustainable health of the corporation, and the protection of its independence and its jobs.

It is now widely recognized that businesses need to focus on corporate-value creation to remain economically viable and independent. This refocus from revenue growth to value creation is not just a matter of words—it requires a substantial transformation for established corporations.

Ultimately, this transformation is really achieved when the concept of "corporate-value creation" becomes part of the business culture. This means when it has become a belief or value shared by employees of the organization, joining other beliefs and values that composed the business culture cumulatively over time, such as customer centricity. When it becomes part of the culture, decisions and behaviour become more naturally aligned toward a common goal. This is the case, as we mentioned earlier, in firms born in the new economy and that already have corporate-value creation in their DNA.

For an established firm to acquire this new, shared belief takes leadership, time, and massive communication and training. But it can be done and is actually an unescapable avenue for all corporations if they want to survive in the long term.

Many businesses are engaged in a *digital transformation*. This is most relevant in today's environment, but it is only one component of the more fundamental *corporate-value creation transformation*. Digitalization is essential for any business today. But the real transformation is creation of corporate value, and digitalization is only one dimension of that change. Its success will not be measured on its technological achievements but on its contribution to the creation of corporate value.

So, what does a business transformation for greater corporate-value creation really imply? The pathway to this transformation commonly used by shareholder activists mentioned earlier is to focus on products and markets that have the highest value-creation potential; they will usually divest or sell other activities and reduce all kinds of waste. This approach is also well illustrated by the example of GE which, after a long cycle of acquisitions, focused on corporate-value creation through a large number of divestments, and finally, by splitting the company into three strongly focused businesses.

Such dramatic restructuring of a corporation can achieve substantial short-term gains in corporate value. But to have a sustainable impact, a business transformation for corporate-value creation should engage the whole organization. Indeed, any employee in any department can contribute to corporate-value creation in a variety of ways: elimination of waste, improved product quality, increased efficiencies, more and better innovations, improved customer service, more lucrative sales, greater business development, or enhanced reputation, among many others. It also confers benefits to all contributing employees by creating a healthy, stable, and stimulating work environment. In addition, it should eventually lead to compensation benefits such as salary increases or higher incentives.

The transformation of a corporation to focus on corporate-value creation will usually be initiated by top management and coordinated

by the strategy department. But to be successful, it should mobilize
the entire business.

All the support functions such as finance, human resources,
information technology, and administration should contribute to
streamline the organization, increase efficiency, and promote value-
generating actions. The operations functions, including research and
development, procurement, manufacturing, and supply chain management must continuously improve the value-generating capacity
of the company's product portfolio and delivery system. Marketing
needs to improve the return on investment of its actions and to concentrate on value-generating activities. And sales has to enhance its
value-capture role to contribute to generation of corporate value,
as opposed to just focusing on increasing revenues.[3] This means
upholding a higher share of the value created for the customers.

Transforming a business to focus on corporate-value creation
needs to be organized into phases over several years. Priorities must
be set by top management and not all functions and activities will be
affected at the same time. But for all functions, the implications of a
transformation focusing on corporate-value creation can be seen in
two categories:

- **Descaling.** This basically means that some jobs will disappear.
  There are many reasons for this, including suppression of activities, digitalization, or higher efficiencies.
- **Upgrading.** This means that existing jobs will be enriched, or
  that new, higher-level jobs will be created.

In a transformation with a corporate-value creation focus, the
sales function will definitely be subjected to this dual descaling/
upgrading action. The 1st sales transformation, driven by the client

imperative, and the 2nd sales transformation, driven by the marketing/ sales-alignment imperative, were mainly sources of enrichment for sales professionals, usually accompanied by an increase in the size of the sales force.

This 3rd sales transformation is different. On the negative side, the size of some sales forces is likely to be reduced and some sales pros may not be able to tackle the new challenges. On the positive side, it will result in a much higher upgrading of the sales function in which the sales pro will have a broader business perspective and greater responsibilities. This will, however, require a new sales role and new sales skills, in addition to the existing ones.

This transformation is indeed a major challenge for sales professionals as they have to extend their performance into new territories often unfamiliar to them. Among other new capabilities, they must learn how to do the following:

- Acquire a strong financial awareness and business acumen
- Integrate more information into the sales-negotiation process, especially around cost dynamics, contract profitability, and customer satisfaction
- Turn down contracts that destroy value, even if they could generate additional revenue
- Juggle multiple objectives. When you enter the corporate-value creation territory, you not only have to allow for revenue, but also profitability, competitive strength, and customer satisfaction, among other objectives.

Sales professionals are generally not fully aware of the implications of value creation for the corporation, which is a different challenge than value creation for the customer. Once you develop this, you will find you are better prepared to step up to this new territory of capturing corporate value and are able to deliver greater value not only to your customers, but also to the corporation you work for.

THE DRIVERS OF CORPORATE-VALUE CREATION

Knowing the origin, rationale, and context for this 3rd sales transformation, you may now be asking yourself how to recognize if you contribute to corporate-value creation.

Corporate-value creation corresponds to any activity that increases the worth of a corporation, and it is essential for you to identify what drives your corporate-value creation capability. These drivers can be specific to different corporations, such as securing sources of supplies, technologies, or talents. But, as we have already seen in several examples, three elements stand out as key corporate-value creation drivers across all business sectors:

Profitability. The capacity of a corporation to generate profits—in the short, medium, and long term—is the most obvious driver of its value. The current profitability of a corporation is easy to quantify, and it is the most-immediate indicator of the business's future profitability. But focusing only on current profitability would privilege short-term actions and could even lead to corporate-value destruction.

Market share. When a corporation has a larger share of a market, one can expect that its future profitability will increase for several reasons. It will generate economies of scale that reduce costs. It will have more power with clients, distributors, and partners, which will allow it to benefit from higher prices. Market share is an important driver of medium- and long-term corporate value.

Customer satisfaction. Higher customer satisfaction leads to repeat purchases and increased retention, reputation, recommendations, and other factors that have a positive impact on corporate-value creation. Building on happy, existing customers is a much easier and more sustainable way to build a business than constantly struggling to bring in new leads to replace lost customers. Customer satisfaction is thus a fundamental driver of long-term corporate-value creation. Businesses that create value in the short term by sacrificing customer satisfaction invariably see their corporate value eroded over the long term.

In this book, we concentrate on these three key drivers of value creation for three main reasons:

- They are the ones most supported by research on corporate-value creation in a wide range of sectors
- They provide a balance for companies looking to create value over the short, medium, and long term
- They are the ones on which the sales force can and should have an impact

I have listed these drivers in the specific order of profitability, market share, and customer satisfaction because this is the most common order of priority in established corporations. Different companies will, however, place different priorities and weights on each of these drivers. As a sales pro, you should be aware of these weights, and in a company focusing on corporate-value creation, your incentives will most likely be tied to these weights.

It is often said that before you attempt to take on a new challenge you should ask yourself several times, "Why?"—drilling down to the root cause of the issue and the essence of your motivation. The purpose of the first three chapters of this book is to respond to these *why* questions, to give you the background and rationale for the 3rd sales transformation, and the self-confidence to face it. The balance of the book focuses on the *how*, giving you the capabilities and tools you need for the increasingly important second phase of the selling process, to become a value-capture pro and a winner in this 3rd sales transformation.

Absorb and apply the lessons you learn, because your future— and the future of your business—depend on it.

CHAPTER 4

MASTERING MULTIPLE OBJECTIVES

"Hello, Mr. Martin—have I got a great offer for you!"

You would probably agree with me that this is not the right way to start most sales encounters today, especially complex ones, though it has been used quite effectively for centuries by merchants and salespeople of all types.

As we saw in Chapter 2, today's modern selling approach focuses on the creation of perceived customer value, which requires first investigating the customer's needs. This is the first phase of a customer encounter. Selling for corporate-value creation—the focus of this book—is the second phase of a customer encounter, and it leads to closure on a favourable transaction. But before entering this determining phase, one needs to make sure that the customer or prospect has a favourable perception of the value of our offer.

Just as a reminder, before we focus on corporate-value creation, the various steps in the first selling phase should look something like this:

- Establish a relationship with the customer
- Investigate the customer's context and needs by taking a consultative approach
- Present the offer, focusing on value relative to the customer's needs
- Manage questions and objections
- Refocus on perceived customer value to boost WTP (willingness to pay)

The objective of this first selling phase is to convince the customer that the offer is most attractive relative to their needs, and to generate a high WTP before entering into the second selling phase, which centres on negotiations.

The second selling phase can proceed with the same person or with a different one, depending on the situation. In large client companies, and for major items, it is indeed likely that different people will participate in the purchasing process, and they can be organized into three distinct groups:

- **Prescribers** define the desired specifications and evaluate the proposed offer
- **Users** are those who will actually benefit from the offer if it is acquired
- **Buyers** make the final decision and specify the terms of the transaction.

Most frequently, the person with a prescribing role (e.g., product specialist, engineering, manufacturing, department head) will be the key contact in the first phase, and the person with the buying role (e.g., procurement officer, department head, CEO) will be the key contact in the second phase. Users may be consulted in the first phase but are unfortunately often neglected despite their important influence for repeat purchases.

For simple purchased goods and services, or in small firms, the same person may play all three roles. For more-complex situations, the members of these three groups will depend on the nature of the purchase. In the case of computer equipment, for example, the prescriber is usually the IT department, possibly supported by external experts. The users are employees throughout the organization who depend on the computer equipment to do their work, and the buyers are officers in the procurement department.

In the case of large-scale computerized management processes, the prescribers are frequently top executives—often in collaboration with an external specialized company—and the IT department. The users are practically all employees in the company, and the buyers are the CEO and the executive committee, with the support of the procurement department.

As you can see, maximizing your effectiveness in the second selling phase requires knowing who the decision makers are, ensuring they are aware of the value that you will provide to their business, and addressing any questions they may have.

MOVING FROM THE FIRST SELLING PHASE TO THE SECOND SELLING PHASE

The first phase of a selling encounter, centred on customer value, is specific to the offer and the type of customer. In Chapter 2, we explored an example of a firm manufacturing electronic devices. Based on a market segmentation analysis, the recommendations made by marketing to emphasize customer value were different for three customer groups: "The Privileged Partner" for large enterprises, "The Full-Service Solution" for medium enterprises, and "The Easy Option" for small enterprises. Based on these preliminary guidelines, sales pros can prepare for their client encounter by developing a customer-value selling strategy and adapting it during their interactions with the customer.

Customer-value selling works only if it is specifically adapted to the product or service being sold and to the individual prospect or client. As you can imagine, selling a portfolio of consumer goods produced by Coca-Cola, PepsiCo, or Mondelez to the purchasing manager of the beverage department of a retailer is a quite different situation than selling airbags to senior buyers of automobile manufacturers such as Ford or BMW.

It should therefore be no surprise that the profile of the sales pros recruited for these different jobs is totally different, and so too is their training in terms of products and services offered. While the general customer-value selling approach remains the same across this broad spectrum, its application is specific to each market, and the training of sales pros requires a significant adaptation of the selling techniques to the sector in which they operate.

The second phase of the sales process involves negotiations where the sales pro focuses on obtaining an agreement that is both acceptable to the client and maximizes corporate-value creation. The principles of value-capture selling that I present in this book are similar over the entire spectrum of situations mentioned for customer-value selling—from selling consumer goods to the purchasing manager of a retailer's beverage department, to selling airbags to the senior buyers of automobile manufacturers.

In addition, value-capture selling concentrates on the financial aspects of the agreement and not on the specifications of the offer, which are usually determined in the first phase. It is thus much less dependent on context than customer-value selling. Training for value-capture selling does not need to be customized as much as training for customer-value selling, but it does require a much deeper and more rigorous understanding of financial matters. Let's take a deeper dive into some of these financial considerations.

REVENUE MANAGEMENT SYSTEMS AND THE VALUE-CAPTURE CULTURE

In some situations, navigating through all the options available to choose from when putting together an offer for a client can be very complex. Just visualize the task of a sales pro in the beverage industry facing the purchasing manager of a retail chain with:[1]

- More than 30 brands, including a market-brand leader essential for all retailers, many mature brands, and some new brands that need to be referenced to have a chance to establish a position
- A total of more than 300 SKUs (stock keeping units) including different variations, containers, and sizes
- Different profitability for each SKU
- Guidelines from sales management to favour the association of selected groups of brands in the purchasing agreement
- Priorities to obtain placement of certain specific brands in the stores

In addition to the complexity inherent in a broad portfolio, the sales pro will have to face a variety of requests for special discounts, promotional allowances, donations to various events, and many other contributions imagined by the purchasing department to improve the value of the agreement to the retail store.

To help sales pros cope with such complexity, many firms have developed *revenue management systems*. These software-driven systems—usually accessible on a tablet to prepare for a sales meeting or to interact more effectively during a negotiation[2]—provide instant information along with an evaluation of a proposed deal and guidance for improving it. The objective of these systems, without naming it, is definitely to support *value capture*.

Revenue management systems originated in the hospitality and airline industries to modulate prices on different days and times according to occupancy. As consumers, we are very familiar with these systems, which increase prices dynamically as the number of available hotel rooms or airline seats decreases.

In most sectors, the nature of the products and services, and the relationships with customers, do not warrant a revenue management system. And when it *is* used, a revenue management system, while valuable, may have a pernicious double effect. The first effect is to relieve sales pros from having to make the effort to dive into some fundamental financial issues. The second effect is to take some personal responsibility away from sales pros as the outcome of an agreement can sometimes be blamed on the unavoidable limits of the system. Both of these outcomes can have a negative impact on corporate-value creation.

These pernicious effects can be avoided by developing a *value-capture spirit*, ensuring the continuous ownership of the process by the sales pros, whatever support system they are provided with. It is this spirit which will contribute to developing a culture that will naturally drive corporate-value creation, as mentioned in Chapter 3. The development of such a value-capture spirit is not provided by a system. It requires a deep understanding by sales pros of the corporate-value creation issues, so that they can master them and build their self-confidence.

NEGOTIATING ACCORDING TO INCENTIVES

Sales pros sell and negotiate with clients to reach the objectives given to them by management, and in the process maximize their incentives and income. Management sets incentives rules to align sales behaviour with company objectives. If, for example, a car dealer wants to quicky clear its parking lot of last year's models, it will offer salespeople a significant boost on the commission they receive when they sell those particular cars.

The 3rd sales transformation's focus on creating corporate value requires new sales-incentive systems. As a result, sales pros will have to develop a stronger business acumen and the ability to juggle multiple objectives, as introduced in Chapter 3. This is not about understanding all the intricacies of financial analysis, but instead to develop a level of dexterity with numbers that will allow you to have the proper reflexes in a negotiation and to build your self-confidence.

Let's start with the simplest of situations and build toward more-complex ones in the context of corporate-value creation as we review three commonly used sales objectives: volume, revenue, and profitability.

THE VOLUME OBJECTIVE

Depending on the industry, the *volume* of a product or service that a sales pro tries to negotiate with a client can be expressed in a variety of ways, such as units, thousands of units, cases, crates, tons, cubic meters, staff-hours, staff-days, staff-months, gigawatt hours, or more.

It is rare that sales pros are given a single volume sales objective— say, to sell a minimum of 1,000 cases of a soft-drink brand by a certain date—as this has the potential to be less than optimal to the company. Indeed, the risk is that sales pros will *always* give away the maximum discount allowed to achieve a faster deal and meet the volume sales objective. This is why such a simplistic objective is given only in limited cases, for example, to clear a warehouse of lingering stocks or to more quickly fill a newly created manufacturing capacity.

This is the simplest negotiating situation, and one may indeed think that the easiest deal is for the sales pro to immediately give customers the maximum price discount allowed by management— quickly securing a sale. It is certainly true that if the sales pro has an incentive based only on volume, then he or she has no personal interest in wasting time negotiating a higher price that will not contribute to his or her income.

Can you pause and think of at least three reasons why this may not be the case? Why even in this simplest situation the sales pro should first try to obtain the highest volume, but also at the highest possible price for that volume?

The first reason, and in my view, the most important one, is that a professional salesperson, in addition to preserving his or her personal income, should continuously strive to obtain the best possible sales deal for his or her company. This is a matter of pride and self-development essential for the long-term success of any sales pro.

The second reason is that revealing the feasibility of the low price resulting from a maximum discount will make future negotiations with the same client more difficult. They will always want the maximum discount, and they may be upset when you don't continue to offer it. Or they may simply seek out a different supplier that will honour the discount.

The third reason is that a low price given to a customer may through various networks be discovered by other customers and then be used as a precedent. They will, of course, want the same low price you granted to the first customer, and you may be hard pressed to explain why you won't offer it to these other customers.

While a single volume objective is the most simplistic selling situation possible, it demonstrates that even in such a case, the role of the thoughtful sales pro is crucial. A support system should indeed facilitate the tasks of sales pros, but they cannot replace the *value-capture spirit* that is an essential part of the corporate-value culture.

THE REVENUE OBJECTIVE

Revenue is the most commonly used objective in sales forces over a broad range of sectors, and incentives are usually expressed as a percentage of revenues invoiced. There are many variations to this scheme, with or without a base salary, with or without thresholds, and other modalities. But the main principle is that sales pros receive a commission, usually equal to 2–25 percent of net revenues invoiced, often adjusted by returns or unpaid invoices.

This is a very simple scheme, but more realistic than one based strictly on volume as it takes into account the actual price of the transaction, and hence the discount granted. Under this scheme, a sales pro aiming to optimize his or her commission should consider granting an additional discount only if it would result in an increase in revenue that would more than compensate for that discount.

While the revenue scheme is simple to understand, appraising the willingness of a buyer to buy more for an extra discount is not easy. Also keep in mind that when they are in an uncertain situation, most sales pros would prefer a bad deal to no deal at all.

Even with perfect information, however, the best agreement for the sales pro is not always intuitively obvious. Let's take a simple example where Joan, a sales professional, is negotiating an agreement for a yearly contract with Nancy, a buyer for a large retail chain. Joan offers to sell a product to Nancy with the following commercial guidelines from her sales manager: List price of $10 per box for a minimum of 10,000 boxes, meaning an order of $100,000, with a maximum allowed discount of 50 percent beyond this minimum order. This maximum allowed discount is undisclosed by Joan and unknown to Nancy.

To obtain a better deal, Nancy reveals her simple purchasing plan to Joan. She needs more than the minimum quantity of 10,000 boxes and would order an additional 4,000 boxes for each extra $1 of discount offered by Joan. This is an uncommon situation where Joan has perfect information, but even in this case, the best agreement is not intuitive for the sales pro. You can experience this for yourself by stepping back to see how much time it takes for you to find an appropriate response, even one that is approximate.

Joan first considers that if she gives a discount of $1, Nancy will buy 14,000 boxes at $9, resulting in an order for $126,000—making the discount very worthwhile. Considering further discounts, Joan realizes that with a discount of $4, Nancy would buy 26,000 boxes at $6 for an order of $156,000. For a greater discount of $5, the potential order would fall to $150,000—a decline in revenue. Thus, the best agreement for Joan is a $4 discount that leads to a $156,000 order (see Table 4.1).

Table 4.1   Optimizing a revenue objective.

	Volume (boxes)	Discount ($)	Price ($)	Order size ($)
Deal 1	10,000	0	10	100,000
Deal 2	14,000	1	9	126,000
Deal 3	18,000	2	8	144,000
Deal 4	22,000	3	7	154,000
Deal 5	**26,000**	**4**	**6**	**156,000**
Deal 6	30,000	5	5	150,000

If you tried to work out a solution to this problem, I suspect you would have to admit that this appropriate response is not intuitively obvious, even with perfect information. In practice, seller and buyer would find their way to a mutually agreeable outcome through an iterative process, without divulging the entire scope of their possibilities. As a result, as many sales professionals realize, the agreement reached with a buyer is often not optimum but is hopefully satisfactory enough to achieve their goals, and their company's goals.

THE PROFITABILITY OBJECTIVE

While the revenue sales objective is simple to comprehend and the most commonly used, it is part of the era of revenue growth at all costs that led to widespread corporate-value destruction, as we saw in Chapter 3. A *profitability* objective, on the other hand, is more aligned with a focus on the creation of corporate value, at least in the short term. As profitability is lower than revenues, the commission rates are in this case naturally set higher than the ones used for revenues and depend on the profit level of the product or service offered.

There are, however, three concerns with a profitability objective. Fortunately, all three of these concerns are quite solvable.

The first concern is that it requires communicating financial information to sales pros, with the fear that this information could be misused or widely spread among customers or prospects. In my view, this fear is the symptom of a corporate pathology that needs to be cured as quickly as possible.

As we saw earlier, high corporate performance requires that value creation be shared by all, and this requires a minimum level of financial information. This information, and often much more, is readily accessible in published annual reports, on the internet, and is provided by financial analysts to justify their recommendations.

The fear of disclosure—and the secrecy that results—are thus a very disconcerting sign that management puts more trust in outsiders than it does in the company's employees. Any effective corporate culture must be based on trust, and providing adequate financial information to sales pros is an important element of this trust.

The second concern is that the estimation of profitability requires the selection of the exact cost to be used in the sales process. There are various kinds of costs, including fixed costs (that do not change with volume) and variable costs (that do change with volume). There are also direct costs (linked to a specific activity), indirect costs (not directly associated with an activity), and other ways of classifying costs.

The cost to be considered in the calculation of profitability for sales must be clear and simple enough to enable action, as opposed to wasting time and energy on fruitless discussions. The most common approach is to use a unit cost based on the variable costs of delivering one unit of the product or service considered, plus an allocation of fixed costs as well as a minimum margin. The accuracy of such a unit cost can always be contested, but what is important is that the behaviour that it creates is aligned with the corporate objective.

The third concern is that profitability as an objective is not as simple as revenues and may be scary for some sales pros who are fearful of financial matters. This may sometimes be true, especially if the transition to a profitability objective is imposed hastily without proper explanation and training. In my experience, however, sales pros are much more capable of mastering their own finances—including incentives and expenses—than are many corporate managers. This concern will be totally resolved with proper training and the use of a sales-support software package readily available on a tablet or smartphone, with instant access to financial data and swift calculation of the profitability implications of a proposed deal.

To understand the implications of moving from revenues to profitability as a sales objective, let's go back to the meeting between Joan, the seller, and Nancy, the buyer.

With the same commercial guidelines—minimum quantity, list price, and maximum allowable discount—Joan is now told that her commission will be a percentage of the profitability of the agreements she negotiates. She is thus incentivized to maximize this profitability. The additional information she is given is that the unit cost of the product sold is $5 per box.

On her side, Nancy still indicates that she needs more than the minimum quantity of 10,000 boxes, and that she would order an additional 4,000 boxes for each extra $1 of discount. So, the only difference with the previous sales situation is that profitability is the objective rather than revenues.

How different do you think the optimum volume is for which Joan should negotiate a deal?

Joan first understands that at the minimum quantity of 10,000 boxes and a price of $10, she would show a profit of $50,000. With a discount of $1, volume would increase to 14,000 boxes and profit to $56,000, making the discount worthwhile. For a discount of $2, volume increases to 18,000 boxes and profit drops to $54,000. Using the support software issued to her by her company, Joan can further refine these estimates and find that her optimum deal would be obtained by giving a discount of $1.25 per box and reaching an agreement for 15,000 boxes sold at $8.75, for revenues of $131,250 and a profit of $56,250 (see Table 4.2).

Table 4.2   Optimizing a profitability objective.

	Volume (boxes)	Discount ($)	Price ($)	Revenues ($)	Unit margin ($)	Profitability ($)
Deal 1	10,000	0	10	100,000	5	50,000
Deal 2	14,000	1	9	126,000	4	56,000
Deal X	**15,000**	**1.25**	**8.75**	**131,250**	**3.75**	**56,250**
Deal 3	18,000	2	8	144,000	3	54,000
Deal 4	22,000	3	7	154,000	2	44,000
Deal 5	26,000	4	6	156,000	1	26,000

As you can see, the outcome of the sale is very different with this profitability objective than with the revenue objective: the volume sold has gone down from 26,000 to 15,000 boxes, about 35 percent. Because of the lower discount, revenues have dropped less, by 16 percent, from $156,000 to $131,250. But profit for 26,000 boxes was only $26,000, with a discounted price of $6 for a unit cost of $5. For only 15,000 boxes sold, however, profit is $56,250. With a profitability objective, the value captured has more than doubled, with 40 percent less volume!

This is a compelling demonstration of how a focus on corporate value can provide *more for less*, a much more efficient use of the company resources! This is also a very simple, but realistic and telling example of value destruction described in the previous chapter. By focusing on revenues instead of profitability, Joan would have destroyed more than half of the potential corporate value that could have been created with her customer, Nancy.

BEYOND THE PROFITABILITY OBJECTIVE

As you can see, the profitability objective is a positive step toward the creation of corporate value. However, in addition to the three concerns about profitability objectives mentioned above, the objective suffers from an important shortcoming: it privileges the short-term aspect of corporate value at the expense of its medium- and long-term dimensions.

Let's go back once again to the negotiations between Joan, the seller, and Nancy, the buyer. While Nancy had revealed her purchasing plan in terms of volume relative to price, she had not disclosed her anticipated yearly need for this product category. If I now tell you that Nancy needs to secure a total of 50,000 boxes for the year, this should shed a new light on the deal for 26,000 boxes reached with the revenue objective versus the 15,000 boxes deal with the profitability objective. What do you think?

With a volume of 26,000 boxes, Joan's firm would capture a 52 percent share of Nancy's firm in this category and would be its primary supplier, gaining a powerful relationship as a strategic partner. With a volume of 15,000 boxes, however, Joan's firm would only have a 30 percent share of Nancy's firm in this category and would be at best a secondary, or possibly a tertiary, supplier. This would likely deprive Joan's firm of privileged information and reduce its chances of a favourable agreement in the coming years.

The risk is that having a single profitability objective may jeopardize medium- and long-term corporate-value creation. This could be avoided by aiming for an agreement with a volume level in between those obtained with the single revenue or profitability objectives. Maybe 22,000 boxes, which would result in a $44,000 profit and a 44 percent share of Nancy's needs? Favouring a volume under or above this midpoint should depend on the requirement of Joan's firm for short- versus medium- and long-term value.

Another factor influencing the medium- and long-term corporate value created by the agreement negotiated by Joan is how satisfied Nancy is by the agreement. Indeed, Nancy's satisfaction in her relationship with Joan will affect her disposition to buy this or other products from Joan's firm in the future. Clearly, Nancy would be more satisfied with a higher discount and a volume that would secure a higher portion of her needs, while leaving room for some other suppliers to provide variety and reduce risks. But Nancy's satisfaction will also be affected by other aspects, including the negotiation process itself. Unlike profitability and revenues, satisfaction is not a quantitative concept and is more complex to understand. We will thus devote the entire Chapter 5 to better master it.

With the example of this encounter between Joan, the sales professional, and Nancy, the buyer, we have progressively introduced and illustrated the three drivers of corporate-value creation that we mentioned in Chapter 3: profitability, market share, and customer satisfaction. You can now better appreciate how a singular focus on revenues can lead to corporate-value destruction and how a singular focus on profitability can lead to short-termism.

I am sure you now realize that having a single objective made life simpler and that aiming at multiple objectives will require more thought. You are right!

HARNESSING THE THREE DRIVERS OF CORPORATE-VALUE CREATION

With a single objective—volume, revenue, or profitability—it is easy for sales professionals to relate their incentives to potential outcomes: the more the better. And it is thus equally easy for management to align the sales force's behaviour to the volume, revenue, or profitability objectives.

As we have seen, however, such singular objectives can result in corporate-value destruction in the short, medium or long term. This is why winning the 3rd sales transformation requires setting multiple sales objectives in line with the drivers of corporate-value creation.

In this book, we will restrict ourselves to the three commonly used drivers presented in Chapter 3 (profitability, market share, and customer satisfaction) although the same principles apply when different drivers are chosen.

While multiple sales objectives provide the potential to effectively focus on corporate-value creation, they need to be combined into a clear formula so that sales pros know how to maximize their incentives. Such a formula needs to specify:

- The target level for each objective
- The weight of each objective
- The level of bonus granted when meeting these objectives, and its variation for different outcomes

Table 4.3 illustrates an example of such an incentive scheme communicated to Bill, a sales pro at GEN CORP, for one of his large accounts:[3]

The targets indicate clearly what GEN CORP considers a desirable agreement to be for this account in terms of the three objectives. In addition to the $100,000 profitability target, in this case, the firm accepts being a minor supplier with a 20 percent share of the customer's business and would be happy with a 70 percent customer satisfaction rating.[4] If Bill delivers on these targets, he will receive a $15,000 bonus for this account.

Table 4.3 Example of a corporate-value incentive scheme.

	Profitability	Market share (%)	Customer satisfaction (%)	Bonus
Target	$100,000	20	70	$15,000
Weight (%)	50	30	20	100

As Bill is unlikely to hit these targets exactly, the weights indicate what trade-offs he should favour as he negotiates with his client. GEN CORP would prefer that he meets all three targets, but it clearly gives more importance to profitability, with a weight (50 percent) that is equal to the combined weights for market share and customer satisfaction. This weighting scheme may be in place because the company's executive team decided that a stronger focus on short-term profitability was necessary at the time.

If GEN CORP as cash-rich, it might have taken the opportunity to favour greater investments in market share and customer satisfaction to secure continued corporate-value creation in the medium and long term. In this case, the weights given to profitability, market share, and customer satisfaction could have been, for example, 30 percent, 40 percent, and 30 percent, respectively.

Bill knows his target objectives and weights for this account, but they do not tell him what bonus he would receive if he underperforms or overperforms on these targets. For instance, if he reached an agreement with $110,000 in profitability, 30 percent market share, and 80 percent customer satisfaction, he should obtain more than his target bonus, having exceeded all three of his objectives. But what do you think his bonus should be?

When I ask this question in sales workshops, the answers I receive range anywhere from just 100 percent to more than 200 percent of bonus! The proper response depends, of course, on the specifics of the bonus scheme put in place by Bill's firm.

The company may decide not to reward any performance above the targets to avoid compensation of a shortcoming in one (e.g., profitability) by a surplus in others (e.g., market share or customer satisfaction), in which case, Bill would receive $15,000. Or it may provide an additional bonus for exceeding the targets, in which case Bill would receive more than $15,000. In any case, the rules relating the incentive to the outcome of an agreement must be clear and they must be established upfront.

At this point, you probably miss the simplicity of a single sales objective and its related commission as an incentive. I understand your feelings here, but fortunately bonus schemes based on multiple objectives are easily implemented thanks to the sales-support software widely available today. Using this support software, for example, Bill can simulate the bonus that he would receive for different outcomes, as shown in Table 4.4.

Bill can see that, given the incentive rules defined by his company, he will receive more than the expected bonus if he exceeds all his targets (Outcome 1). Even if he misses one target, such as for market share in Outcome 3, he can receive more than his expected bonus by delivering above the target for the other two objectives. He can also see in Outcome 2 that he will still receive a bonus if he misses all his targets, so long as the agreement created some corporate value.

Comparing Outcome 4 with Outcome 2, Bill can also see that his firm is rewarding the extra 20 percent of customer satisfaction with an additional 5 percent bonus. Outcome 5 tells him that if he reaches an agreement with a profitability of only $50,000, he will not receive any bonus, even with a market share double the target, as his firm has decided that this result would destroy corporate value.[5]

Table 4.4   Example of bonus alignment with corporate-value outcomes.

	Profitability ($)	Market share (%)	Customer satisfaction (%)	Bonus (%)
Outcome 1	110,000	30	80	120
Outcome 2	90,000	10	60	80
Outcome 3	110,000	10	80	110
Outcome 4	90,000	10	80	85
Outcome 5	50,000	40	70	0

The formula linking the multiple objectives to ensure corporate-value creation, and hence used for bonus determination, must be clearly defined. But, unlike the commission rates for single objectives, such as revenues and profitability, it is not just a percentage and cannot be intuitively determined by sales pros. It can, however, be easily integrated into a sales-support application on a tablet or smartphone.

Sales professionals can easily play with such an app to familiarize themselves with the bonus scheme by simulating different scenarios, just as Bill did. During a sales meeting, the same app will swiftly provide them with a financial evaluation as well as the expected bonus of a potential agreement in a simple dashboard. In addition to understanding what influences their incentives, mastering these multiple objectives provides sales pros with a practical appreciation of their firm's commitment to the healthy development of a value-capture or corporate-value creation culture within the sales force.

UPGRADING THE ROLE OF SALES PROS

The 1st and 2nd sales transformations—improving sales performance through a more effective interface, with clients, on one side, and marketing, on the other—have significantly contributed to the professionalization of the sales function. These transformations concentrate on improving the outcome of the first phase of the encounter between a sales pro and a prospect or client: the creation of customer value and of a significant WTP.

The 3rd sales transformation concentrates on the second phase of the encounter between a sales pro and a prospect or client: the creation of corporate value, or value capture. In this chapter, I introduced the first implication of this transformation: the requirement for multiple objectives to align sales performance on the key drivers of corporate-value creation. This ability to relate and contribute to the broader mission of the firm is key to the performance of sales pros in this new era of focusing on corporate value.

It also implies that sales pros will have to develop their leadership qualities to assume fully their broadened responsibilities, and I develop this idea further in Chapter 6. But in the meantime, let's further explore the corporate-value driver which is the most intangible and most important for the long-term performance of the firm: *customer satisfaction.*

CHAPTER 5

STEERING CUSTOMER SATISFACTION

My friend Sarah is a very busy lawyer who did not take the time to replace her car until the situation had become desperate. She had driven her old clunker for far too long and was tired of constantly having to pour money into it for repairs. So, she decided it was time to bite the bullet and purchase a brand-new vehicle.

Sarah visited several car dealerships in search of the perfect car, but she just couldn't seem to find one that met all her needs and still fit within her budget. That is, until she walked into the showroom of her local Mercedes-Benz dealership and met a salesperson named Lily.

From the moment Sarah met Lily, she could tell that she genuinely cared about helping her find the right car. She listened attentively to her needs and preferences and didn't try to push her into buying something that wasn't a good fit.

Instead, Lily showed her a range of vehicles that met her criteria and gave her honest, straightforward information about each one. She even took the time to explain the different financing options available to her and helped Sarah find a payment plan that worked within her budget.

Sarah was so impressed by Lily's professionalism and kindness that she ended up purchasing a beautiful Mercedes-Benz C-Class from her. She drove off the lot feeling confident that she had made the right decision and grateful for the excellent service Lily provided.

From then on, Sarah made sure to tell all her friends and family about the wonderful experience she had with Lily at the Mercedes-Benz dealership. She even took the time to leave positive reviews on several local social media sites, recommending her salesperson Lily by name. Sarah knew that she would always return to her for any of her future car-buying needs.

We can all relate to the high satisfaction of Sarah in this situation, the quality of the relationship that it creates between her and Lily, and how it eventually impacts positively on the corporate value of Lily's dealership. As consumers, we can intuitively feel the relationship that exists between our satisfaction when shopping in one store and the future success of that store. While less visible, the same pertains to the B2B, business-to-business, world.

In the B2B space, customer satisfaction will directly and positively impact corporate value, as it can help to build strong relationships, leading to increased loyalty and repeat business. Providing a high level of customer satisfaction can also help to improve a company's reputation, which can be beneficial in attracting new customers and partners, again impacting corporate value positively.

Customer satisfaction is the third driver of corporate-value creation. It's different from the first and second drivers—profitability and market share, respectively—in that it is somewhat indefinite and intangible. Customer satisfaction remains only a feeling unless it is measured through specific initiatives. Realizing the importance of customer satisfaction on their development and corporate value, an increasing number of companies have set up programmes to assess customer satisfaction. Many firms, including Salesforce, Zendesk, HubSpot, and Qualtrics, offer a variety of products and platforms that enable B2B companies to measure customer satisfaction. In addition, a number of firms specialize in helping companies design and implement customer satisfaction tracking systems.

So, make no mistake about it—most companies, and the people who run them, are aware of the critical importance of this third driver of corporate-value creation.

Customer Satisfaction and Corporate Value

Customer satisfaction is a key driver of corporate value in two complementary ways: through its impact on profitability and its impact on customer value.

Since the 1980s, it has been widely documented that when customers are satisfied by their transactions with businesses, this leads to increased retention, repeat purchases, increased revenues, positive word of mouth, and various forms of engagement. It is expected that through these cascading effects, customer satisfaction also has a positive impact on profitability. This has been difficult to prove, however, because many other factors (such as the actual price paid for an item or the costs to produce it) have an influence on profitability as well. Fortunately, a number of recent studies have definitively demonstrated a positive relationship between customer satisfaction for a company and its profitability, and this positive effect is now widely accepted.[1]

Beyond its impact on profitability, customer satisfaction is also a driver of corporate value because of its impact on customer value. A company's customer base has been increasingly recognized as one of its most crucial assets. It is not a tangible and internally controlled fixed asset like buildings or machinery, but it is even more important for the long-term value of the company. The concept of *customer life-time value* (CLV) has thus become an important consideration in estimating the value of a corporation.[2]

As its name indicates, CLV reflects the expected value of a customer to a company over the lifetime of the business relationship, calculated as the average annual purchases of a customer, multiplied by the number of years he or she will keep buying from the company. Consider the example of a devoted Starbucks customer who buys 12 grande peppermint mochas every week at a price of $7 each. That's equal to 624 drinks a year at a total price of $4,368. Now, assuming this customer remains loyal to Starbucks, and they keep buying grande peppermint mochas at this same rate for 30 years, that equals a CLV of $131,040! The CLV will, of course, edge even higher over time as prices for coffee-based drinks continue to increase, which they invariably do.

But now, back to the B2B situations that are the focus of this book. Think of one of your clients who bought $75,000 worth of goods and services from you last year. What is the CLV of this customer just for the next 10 years? How will it evolve with rising prices, if this customer's annual purchases grow, or if your firm comes up with new products? Compute the CLV for any of your customers and you will probably realize that the numbers and the importance of CLV are even greater in B2B than for consumer goods.

Customer satisfaction has a positive impact on the two elements of CLV: the average annual customer purchases—happy customers buy more products from their favoured suppliers—and the customer lifetime through higher retention and loyalty. Customer satisfaction is consequently a key determinant of CLV, and with its additional positive impact on profitability, is thus an important long-term driver of corporate value. It is not surprising that financial analysts take it increasingly into account in their evaluations.

MEASURING CUSTOMER SATISFACTION

Various types of customer satisfaction measurement techniques have been used for years, involving mail surveys, personally distributed questionnaires, phone calls, emails, and more. When you were asked to participate in such polls, it's likely you recognized their limits, including ambiguous questions, lack of time to respond properly, hesitation in selecting an adequate response, and limited knowledge, among others.

Yes, customer satisfaction measurement has its limits but, when properly used, can definitely help with the creation of corporate value.

Typical questions in a customer-satisfaction poll are "How satisfied are you with the quality of the product?" or "Did our service meet your expectations?" Let's consider the most commonly used 0–10 scale. If you are told that the result of this survey is 8.2, this is the average of all responses obtained and is called the *average CSAT score* (as you can guess, CSAT stands for *customer satisfaction*).[3]

It's only at the extremes that such ratings represent true customer satisfaction feedback. Customers who give extreme high or low ratings are expressing emotions that are likely to be remembered and lead to positive or negative actions.

Customers who give a 9 or 10 are positively satisfied and are likely to make positive recommendations to others, personally or online. They can develop positive business relationships that lead to the long-term creation of corporate value, and they can be called "champions," "advocates," or "promoters" of your firm. At the other extreme, customers who give a low rating are very unhappy and are likely to spread negative word of mouth. They can be called "detractors" or "desperados."

Customer-satisfaction ratings are most often used at the company or product level, but they are most valuable at specific stages of the *customer journey*. This journey includes all the interactions a customer can have with a company over time and over all channels. These interactions, also called *touchpoints*, are all opportunities to generate customer satisfaction or dissatisfaction experiences, and hence contribute to the creation or destruction of long-term corporate value.

THE CUSTOMER TOUCHPOINT WITH SALES

Now that we better understand why customer satisfaction is a key driver of corporate value, and have had a glance at some different aspects of measurement, let's focus on the one touchpoint we are most concerned with: the interaction of the customer with our firm during the sales process. As a sales pro, it is in this interaction that you can contribute to the creation of corporate value—not only by the agreement you negotiate, but also by the customer satisfaction you generate in the process.

What you do during your customer interactions will definitely influence your company's total customer satisfaction scores. However, what you should personally be most interested in as a sales professional is not your company's overall customer satisfaction statistic, but instead reaching a target satisfaction rating with a specific customer at the end of a sale.

Determining how satisfied you left a customer in your transaction requires asking them to rate their interaction with you. This can be easily accomplished by way of a short call or email from sales management or an external agency after the conclusion or rejection of an agreement. Most often, this direct feedback, based on several questions, is expressed as a customer satisfaction percentage. In today's environment of continuous feedback, most buyers will be happy to respond when the survey firm is totally transparent about the purpose in reaching out to them.

It is best to obtain this information as soon as possible after a customer transaction for multiple reasons. The first reason is that professional buyers are very busy and attend many meetings with a variety of suppliers. Their memory of a specific encounter is likely to be less precise after a while. Another reason is that the faster the contact, the more impressed the buyer will be by the fact that your firm cares about their opinion and the building of a mutually beneficial relationship. The third reason is that prompt feedback is important for a valuable debrief of the encounter that will be useful for the self-development of the sales pro.

Some sales professionals do not view this kind of outreach to their customers positively—they may even resist it, seeing it as an undesirable control on their behaviour. Keep in mind that customer polls on sales calls should *not* be used for evaluation of the behaviour of sales pros who should be free to adapt to their own style the sales techniques favoured by their firm. The goal is to create corporate value, of which customer satisfaction is an important driver. So, sales pros have to be rewarded on this objective as part of their bonus scorecard or dashboard.

As a sales pro, you should not resist such customer polls. Instead, you should welcome any information that helps you improve your approach with your customers—creating corporate value. In addition, the evidence of customer satisfaction that this feedback provides can also be beneficial to your reputation. Accepting such customer satisfaction measurement with enthusiasm will demonstrate your self-confidence and eagerness to improve. And it is a signal that you are happy to jump on the bus of change for corporate-value creation and to win the 3rd sales transformation.

Unlike other customer touchpoints—where the highest customer satisfaction is desirable—you as a sale pro are in a different place. As we saw in Chapter 4, the creation of corporate value requires that you master multiple objectives in your negotiations. You cannot aim for a top rating in customer satisfaction at the expense of profitability and market share—the other two drivers. Your goal is not a top rating, but a given customer satisfaction target, protecting the long-term corporate value of your firm in accordance with the weight given by your firm to this objective.

Customer polls will also alert you to low ratings that express a strong dissatisfaction from customers who, for whatever reason, have become detractors. While they are unlikely to remain your customers, they are likely to communicate their dissatisfaction to others. I prefer to call them *desperados* because of the damage they can do when driven by strong negative emotions. In other words, they have the ability to destroy corporate value, both directly and indirectly.

In such cases, it is critically important to directly address these frustrated customers' issues as soon as possible. Even if a lost sale cannot be recovered, what is important is to allow these customers to share their frustrations, understand the root causes of the underlying problems, and express your honest intention to try to resolve them. The objective is to lessen negative feelings and reduce the likelihood of actions that destroy corporate value. Experience shows that when such a *customer recovery* is achieved, which is unfortunately not always possible, the recovered customers are likely to become even more loyal in the future. This is the case because they had the opportunity to witness for themselves the actual proof that the firm cared about their opinion and their business.

Now, let's see what you can do to help deliver your customer satisfaction targets.

RATIONAL AND EMOTIONAL CUSTOMER SATISFACTION

In Chapter 2, I described the various components of customer value, illustrating the richness of human psychology. Some of these components could be described as rational (features and financials) and others as more elusive (intangibles and emotions). It should therefore be no surprise that the shaping of customer satisfaction contains both rational and emotional elements—reflecting what we humans do.

Rational customer satisfaction is related to the customer reaching his or her objective in the negotiations, that is, the amount of goods needed at a favourable price. It is also related to the fact that the customer is probably incentivized in some way by their own firm to achieve these objectives. Consider the example of Henry, a customer who needs to purchase 1,000 units of a particular product for the year. Henry would like to divide the 1,000 units between two different suppliers—buying 70 percent from the lead supplier and 30 percent from the secondary supplier—at a total average target price below $200 per unit. Henry expects to get a lower price of around $190 from the lead supplier and $220 from the secondary supplier.

Henry will, of course, not communicate his purchase plan and objectives to the suppliers' sales professionals, although he will provide some hints as the negotiations unfold. The sales pros will not know Henry's satisfaction with an agreement until it is finalized, but one can expect that his rational satisfaction will depend on how closely the final agreement matches his objectives.

If you are retained as the key supplier, obviously, Henry will be quite satisfied from a rational perspective if he obtains 700 units from you at $190 each. But he will be even more satisfied if he obtains the same quantity from you at \$185 each. He will be less satisfied if you insist that he needs to buy 800 units to get the \$190 price, or if you tell him that you cannot go lower than \$195 for a quantity of 700 units. Although you do not know Henry's exact goals during the negotiations, you should expect that his rational satisfaction will move in these directions.

Rational customer satisfaction thus derives from a tangible evaluation of the buying conditions obtained compared to the customer's objectives. All other elements that influence customer satisfaction and are not rationally related to the customer's objective comprise *emotional customer satisfaction*. These elements arise mainly from the customer's conversational interactions, the negotiation process, and from the customer's nonrational reactions to some outcomes.

It is thus important to pay attention to the following elements that can impact the emotional side of a customer's satisfaction, especially in the second phase of the sales process focused on value capture:

- Being attentive to the initial introduction because the first impression has an important influence on perception
- Showing interest in the person as an individual and not just as a sales goal
- Establishing rapport and building strong relationships
- Consistently doing what you say you're going to do
- Being honest and transparent
- Carefully responding to questions and objections
- Establishing and maintaining trust
- Maintaining a consistently respectful and attentive behaviour

Let me describe something I once witnessed on a call with Karen, a sales pro I was shadowing to gather short case studies for a sales training workshop. The call was with Mr. Norwall, a professional buyer at a company in which Karen had for the first time succeeded in having a new product approved by engineering. The meeting had been scheduled for 60 minutes to allow sufficient time to negotiate the terms of a potential agreement, and Karen had shared with me that Mr. Norwall had the reputation of being a tough negotiator.

After the usual introductions, Karen noticed a photograph on the wall. The photo was of Mr. Norwall at the helm of an attractive sailing boat, with all the sails set and a beautiful blue spinnaker fully blown. Karen, an occasional sailor herself, asked Mr. Norwall where this picture had been taken. After a while, they started exchanging their personal views on various boat makers and models, along with their favourite sailing destinations.

Eventually, Mr. Norwall kindly interrupted this animated exchange and asked Karen to talk to him about what she was proposing for this new product. This led to a very frank and cordial discussion at the end of which an agreement was easily reached that was satisfactory for both parties.

I was impressed to witness how Karen had handled the entire meeting, which remained within the planned 60 minutes. The time taken for the more social discussion at the beginning of the encounter was actually compensated for by an easier negotiation. A crucial turning point for the success of this meeting was when Karen noticed the photo of Mr. Norwall on his boat. Be it a picture, a trophy, a diploma, or a book, the things that people display in their office have some importance to them. Not noticing these things shows a lack of interest in the person and a selfish interest in just making the sale. Noticing them is a demonstration of respect and creates positive emotions.

Beyond the conversational interactions, and a rational evaluation of the outcome of a negotiation, the customer's satisfaction will also be influenced by the way this outcome has been reached. Let me share two examples with you, with the first concerning the length of the negotiations. Consider two possible negotiation scenarios:

- Scenario A: The purchaser obtains an 8 percent price reduction after a 10-minute negotiation
- Scenario B: The purchaser obtains a 5 percent price reduction after 30 minutes of tough negotiation

Which of these two scenarios do you think will produce higher customer satisfaction?

Feel at ease, whatever your response is. There is indeed no definitive right or wrong answer to this question, as it will depend on the purchaser and on the situation. However, *on average* (and this is based on a great deal of testing and research), the customers in Scenario B will derive the higher level of satisfaction. Why? Because their emotional satisfaction of having "won" a discount after 30 minutes of tough negotiation will be higher than that of the customers in Scenario A who had an easier win.

Let's now look at the second example, this one concerning the domination of the negotiation process by one or the other party. Again, consider two possible negotiation scenarios:

- Scenario A: After 20 minutes of negotiation that the purchaser dominates, a 5 percent price reduction is accepted by the seller
- Scenario B: After 20 minutes of negotiation that the seller dominates, the purchaser obtains a 6 percent price reduction

Now, which of these two scenarios do you think will produce higher customer satisfaction?

As with the previous example, there is no definitive right or wrong answer. However, on average, the purchasers in Scenario A would feel a greater level of satisfaction than the purchasers in Scenario B. In this instance, it is because of the emotional satisfaction the purchaser in Scenario A will feel as a result of having "won" the negotiation by dominating the process. The rational satisfaction would be higher for the purchaser in Scenario B, but it is the emotional satisfaction that once again wins out, on average.

Rational or emotional, you should not wait for a poll after the close of a sales negotiation to discover how satisfied a customer is. But it is also not feasible to ask a customer directly during the sales process. So, the solution is to train yourself to observe signals of customer satisfaction or dissatisfaction during the process and adjust your actions accordingly. You must become a close observer of human behaviour, and of your customers' verbal and nonverbal communication.

DETECTING CUSTOMER-SATISFACTION SIGNALS

We all communicate our satisfaction and dissatisfaction continuously during our interactions with one another, whether in business or everyday life. It's part of human behaviour, and the importance of self-expression has been well documented in psychology and as a therapeutic instrument.[4] Our innate need to communicate our satisfaction and dissatisfaction to others is well demonstrated by the remarkably fast spread of emoticons and emojis, which add life to otherwise sterile digital communication made through computers, smartphones, and on social media.

Psychologists distinguish between verbal and nonverbal communication, with nonverbal signals often given more weight and prominence than verbal signals. This finding is primarily based on the work of psychologist Albert Mehrabian, who found that 55 percent of communication is facial, 38 percent is vocal (*how* you say something), and 7 percent is verbal (the words themselves).[5] Thus, according to Mehrabian's work, only 7 percent of communication is verbal, while 93 percent is nonverbal—the body language, gestures, and other cues we deliver to convey meaning.

The numbers reported by Mehrabian have been the subject of much debate in the field, especially in terms of the methodologies he used in his research, and they probably underrepresent the average importance of verbal communication. (Unless you're using sign language, it's not easy to communicate with someone who is standing in front of you without speaking, regardless of the vigour of your gestures!) But no expert disputes the critical importance of nonverbal communication which is underestimated by most people.

You should of course be attentive to verbal and nonverbal signals, in all kinds of interactions, whether they are face to face, virtual, or written. But because they weigh so heavily in our interactions, be sure to look closely for the nonverbal signals that your counterpart is sending to you (and also be aware of the nonverbal signals *you* are sending!). Some of the most common forms of nonverbal communication include:

- **Body language.** This includes things like posture, gestures, facial expressions, and eye contact. For example, our facial expressions convey a wide range of emotions and attitudes, such as happiness, sadness, anger, and surprise.
- **Appearance.** This includes clothing, hairstyle, grooming habits, and overall appearance, which can convey information about a person's personality, social status, and cultural background.

- **Proximity.** This refers to the physical distance between people, which can convey information about their relationship and level of comfort with each other, and signal intimacy, aggression, or dominance.
- **Touch.** This includes handshakes, hugs, patting someone on the back, and other physical contact, which can convey a range of meanings, including affection, power dynamics, and social status.
- **Voice.** This refers to the tone, pitch, pacing, and volume with which you deliver your words—these can convey emotions and attitudes.
- **Time.** The way a person uses time, including punctuality and the length of time they devote to an activity (including their meetings with you!), can convey information about their values and priorities.
- **Objects.** The way a person uses objects, such as their choice of phone or their use of certain types of technology, can convey information about their personality and values.

Customer satisfaction signals are richest when you are face to face with your counterpart. This is where you can hear every word and sense for yourself the entirety of someone's nonverbal communication. This is clearly the ideal situation for sales pros.

The signals are weaker in virtual interactions, such as on Zoom, Teams, or other online video platforms in ubiquitous use today (and especially so since COVID-19). While you can hear every word (assuming the internet connections are good ones, which is never a 100 percent certainty these days), you don't get the full richness of nonverbal communication since cameras are usually centered close-up on people's faces. This instead accentuates facial nonverbal signals while cutting out or canceling many others. Note that *not* using a camera in virtual communication is a big negative in a sales situation because it's impossible to read the facial cues of the person who is hiding, potentially undermining trust.

And, of course, customer satisfaction signals are weaker yet when you're interacting strictly in writing, such as via email or communications platforms such as Slack. However, the liberal use of emojis, emoticons, exclamation points, and capital letters can supplement the actual words used.

Like poker players, professional buyers are trained to hide their emotions and to manage their verbal and nonverbal signals. However, it takes a top actor to play another persona, and that top actor needs a good script. In an everyday interaction between people, however, there is no set script, and reactions to unexpected prompts will often produce verbal or nonverbal signals—even from well-trained buyers. As they say, "What's bred in the bone will come out in the flesh." These signals reveal the person's state of mind and detecting them will help you navigate the path to your customer-satisfaction target.

Aiming at the Customer-Satisfaction Target for Corporate Value

In this chapter, I provided you with a deeper understanding of customer satisfaction as a driver of corporate value—its rational and emotional components, and the contribution you can make at the sales touchpoint of the customer journey.

As we will see later, you need to be well prepared before entering any sales negotiation process. But there is only so much you can do in advance—you will have to adjust your approach continuously based on the verbal and nonverbal signals that you detect from buyers during each of their moves and as they react to each of your own. You will also have to manage your own verbal and nonverbal signals according to the information that you want to communicate.

You do all this, and much more, to create as much corporate value as possible. Not just for the customer satisfaction driver that was the focus of this chapter, but also for the other two drivers of corporate value: profitability and market share.

You have probably realized that with multiple objectives combining the short, medium, and long term, your role as a sales pro has been upgraded. Yes, to win the 3rd sales transformation, you need to develop specific leadership capabilities. We cover those leadership capabilities in Chapter 6.

CHAPTER 6

THE LEADERSHIP ATTITUDE

"I enjoyed our meeting, John, but I must conclude that your offer is not our preferred solution. Our requirements may evolve, and we should meet again next year. No need to call me, I will be in touch with you at the proper time."

Having your offer turned down is never a pleasant thing for a sales pro, and you have no doubt found yourself in a similar situation as John, likely more than once or twice, either when prospecting for new clients or serving existing clients. This is why *resilience*—the ability to recover quickly and remain motivated after many rebuttals—is one of the most often-mentioned qualities required of a sales pro.

There are of course others, including such qualities as passion for selling, autonomy, curiosity, energy, drive, conscientiousness, optimism, ambition, mental toughness, and goal-orientation. And these are just a handful of the most commonly cited ones. The lists of required skills found in some sales books are so long that when I look at them, I have the impression that individuals who possess all these skills do not actually exist in the real world. Regardless, these lists are a testament to the fact that selling is a tough job and not suitable for all personalities.

In this chapter, we will not repeat such a list of the traditional qualities required for sales pros—I will assume that you've already got them, or at least know of them. Instead, I will concentrate on the *leadership attitude and behaviour* required by salespeople to succeed in their value-capture mission.

WHY SHOULD YOU BE A LEADER?

When you see the word *leader* used in a business context, it's natural to think about it in terms of someone who is put in charge of a team or organization to lead the people in it—for example, the vice president of sales, or district sales manager, or sales director. In this context, leadership means to be the boss.

However, when I talk about leadership in this chapter, I'm not talking about that. I'm instead talking about your enhanced role as a sales pro with a broader mission to create corporate value.

You have the responsibility to generate corporate value. In this new context, it's as if you are responsible for managing a business made up of your assigned territory with its various clients and prospects. You must feel a sense of ownership in leading this business that you are in charge of and do everything in your power to make its corporate value grow. You should feel the responsibility you have in contributing to the company's good health and to its employees. And you should make it known to your colleagues and boss that you are stepping up to take the lead.

The traditional selling role was all about setting a single objective, developing a short-term orientation, and maintaining a restricted selling task that had little or nothing to do with the strategic mission of the firm. But to win the 3rd sales transformation, that is simply not enough. Not only do you have to *feel* that you are an important part of the implementation of the company strategy, you must *be* an important part of the implementation of the company strategy. And to do this, you must lead your part of the business in line with this strategy.

As we will see in this chapter, developing your leadership skills will also be useful for all your personal interactions (with your clients, marketing, boss, etc.) and for your personal development at work and in your private life.

Still uncertain what I'm talking about? Let's take a deeper dive into the practice of leadership and see how it can help you become a more effective sales professional.

WHAT IS LEADERSHIP?

Leadership guru James MacGregor Burns once said, "Leadership is one of the most observed and least understood phenomena on earth."[1] While I don't agree that it is one of the least understood phenomena on earth, it certainly is one of the most observed, studied, and talked about. Leadership is the most popular subject today in business education, and thousands of books and articles have been written on the topic.[2]

There are a number of issues with these books and articles, including:

- Most are quite general, addressed to those who manage whole organizations, departments, or at least small teams. Seldom do these leadership pieces focus on leading oneself or people not under one's authority.

- Many present impressive lists of qualities required to be an effective leader—10, 20, and sometimes many more. As in the lists of skills required to be an effective sales pro, the impression is you need to be Superman or Superwoman, while in reality, everybody needs to be a leader taking into account one's strengths and weaknesses.

So, what is leadership, and why should you care?

While leadership of the past was steeped in authority and hierarchy, most every modern work emphasizes that leadership is about *social influence*, that is, influencing others *without* exercising authority. Dale Carnegie was a precursor to this leadership approach with his 1936 bestseller, *How to Win Friends and Influence People*, which contained the term "influence people" in its title and is still current today.

There are about as many different definitions of leadership as there are stars in the sky. That said, among the many definitions of leadership available today, I particularly like this simple, straight one by John Maxwell: "Leadership is influence—nothing more, nothing less."[3]

This is the definition that, in my view, focuses on what is at the centre of leadership and most valuable for sales pros who individually, or as part of a team, will win by influencing others without having authority on them: clients, marketing, other colleagues, and their boss. In this book, I focus on the dimensions of leadership most valuable for you, a sales pro faced with the challenge of winning the 3rd sales transformation.

As you have probably observed, leadership has a "hard" and a "soft" side. The hard side focuses mainly on the leadership skills required to perform a task, while the soft side focuses on the human side of the leadership equation. The hard side of leadership is thus the mastery of the required discipline (strategy, marketing, manufacturing, technology, law, and so on), depending on the role of the leader. This is what education traditionally concentrated on. In sales, this mainly concerns selling and negotiating techniques. It is this hard side that gives you the credibility and skills you need to influence others.

With the increased recognition of the importance of leadership skills at all levels, however, it is natural that most leadership courses or books have concentrated on the soft side of leadership, which was long neglected in traditional education. But it is this soft side that gives you the interpersonal skills to influence others, so let's start with that.

THE SOFT SIDE: EMOTIONAL INTELLIGENCE

We all know about IQ—the *intelligence quotient*. The idea of developing a test to compare the intelligence levels of children of the same age came in the early 1900s from French psychologists Alfred Binet and Theodore Simon, and it resulted in the Binet-Simon test. This was later refined by psychologist Lewis Terman in the US who created the Stanford-Binet Intelligence Scale test in 1916. Since then, several forms of tests have been developed and generations of children and adults around the world have been subjected to what became broadly known as *IQ tests*.

IQ tests are still broadly used today, but with more care as their limitations have been recognized over decades of application. Specifically, it has been realized that, rather than providing a direct measurement of innate intelligence, the results are correlated with the ability to take tests, depend on motivation, are affected by the context, and should be adjusted for different cultures. But a major development has been the recognition that many forms of intelligence exist, and that IQ tests mainly measure logic and memory skills.[4] In addition to logic, these different forms of intelligence include, among others, musical, kinesthetic, visual, linguistic, naturalistic, and interpersonal.

It is this interpersonal form of intelligence that has become famous in the field of leadership under the denomination of *emotional intelligence* (EQ). According to its originators, Peter Salovey and John Mayer, emotional intelligence is a set of skills that "contribute to the accurate appraisal and expression of emotion in oneself and in others, the effective regulation of emotion in self and others, and the use of feelings to motivate, plan, and achieve in one's life."[5]

Emotional intelligence explains why in some situations people with high IQ may fail, while others with moderate IQ may succeed. These are generally situations where interpersonal or social skills are important. Individuals with high EQ can indeed better understand and manage emotions—both their own and those of others—which makes them more effective in social settings.

Some individuals have a natural emotional intelligence higher than others. As a sales pro interacting successfully with a variety of people, you probably already have a higher-than-average emotional intelligence. But it can always be improved.

According to psychologist Daniel Goleman, EQ has five components: (1) self-awareness; (2) self-regulation; (3) motivation; (4) empathy; and (5) social skills.[6] But let's better understand what I consider to be the core component of EQ: *empathy*.

AT THE HEART OF EQ IS EMPATHY

Chances are, you have—hopefully rarely—been emotionally assaulted by a salesperson in a shop or market. Not just made uncomfortable, but berated, insulted, and perhaps even screamed at. But do you think that such erratic sales behaviour never happens in professional selling situations? It does, and we all need to be on guard against losing control of our emotions, and ourselves, in our sales negotiations.

Alex had been working as a salesperson with a large client company called Lyon Corp for several years. Lyon was one of Alex's most important B2B customers, and the account was bringing in a significant corporate value for his company. Alex worked hard to build a good relationship with Lyon and successfully closed several major deals with them.

One day, Alex received a call from Lucy, Lyon's purchasing manager, who informed him that they had decided to go with a different vendor for their next order. Alex was shocked and upset by this news, as he thought that everything was going well with the account. He decided to reach out to his main point of contact at Lyon to find out what happened.

When Alex spoke with his contact at Lyon, he found out that the decision was based on price—the other vendor was able to offer a better deal than Alex's company. Alex was angry at Lucy for not giving him a chance to match the price, even suspecting some unethical behaviour, and he called her to express his frustration. Unfortunately, once he got Lucy on the phone, Alex let his emotions get the better of him. He began to shout at her, and said, "You are making a *big* mistake by going with the other vendor. I'm sure you will regret it!"

Lucy was taken aback by Alex's outburst, and she quickly ended the call. Alex's emotional tirade ended up irrevocably hurting his business relationship and Lyon decided not to work with Alex's company in the future—moving all its business to other vendors.

When he had time to take some distance from this unfortunate event, Alex realized that what happened was inexcusable on his part. But there were some special circumstances that led him into this erratic behaviour: he was physically and mentally tired, he had conflicts at that time with his teenage son, he was surprised by the client's decision—the buyer did not give him any signals—and he suspected that his competitor engaged in some unethical practices. He was ashamed of himself and resolved to be more careful in the future. He would never again engage in such erratic behaviour, in any circumstances.

As a sales pro with strong leadership attitude, you should obviously avoid having outbursts of negative emotion that scare or insult others, reduce your credibility, and cause them to seek out other companies to provide the products and services you're selling. This is why the kind of self-awareness and self-regulation mentioned earlier are important. But neither should you become a totally cold and insensitive individual—a robot with no human feelings. This is where empathy comes into the picture.

The ancient Greeks made the distinction between the ideas of *logos* and *pathos*, as introduced by Aristotle in his explanation of rhetoric, or the art of influencing others.[7] *Logos* is influencing through logic and *pathos* is influencing through emotions. Hence the suffix -*pathy* in the words em*pathy* and sym*pathy*.

When you understand the emotions of others and can relate to them, you possess *empathy*. And the greater your empathy, the more you are able to perceive even the mildest expressions of these emotions. If you found yourself in a meeting and witnessed that the person running it did not realize that one of your colleagues was in visible distress, you were empathetic to the fact that the meeting leader had little empathy.

If you share the emotions—for instance, grief, sorrow, anger, or frustration—of someone else, you are expressing *sympathy*. Can you see the difference between sympathy and empathy? When you express *sympathy*, you show that you *share* the other person's emotion, whether you understand it or not. When you express *empathy*, you show that you *understand* the other person's emotion, but you do not necessarily share it.

Most people confuse empathy and sympathy, which can be detrimental because, in business, the distinction between the two is most important. Empathy is essential for understanding emotions, connecting with others, and exercising influence. It involves an *emotional distance* from the person observed to develop an unbiased awareness.

In contrast, when you sympathize with others, you share their feelings and you become *emotionally involved*. While this is quite effective to help somebody in distress, it risks distorting your judgment, which is detrimental to having a good leadership attitude in a business context. This is why empathy is essential for effective leadership, while sympathy goes beyond the limit.

The basic rule is that you should develop your empathy to improve your leadership skills but avoid expressing ongoing sympathy with those who it's your job to influence in a business setting. You can certainly imagine how expressing too much sympathy toward clients, colleagues, or your boss could compromise your position when you try to influence them in a negotiation.

Of course, every rule has exceptions, and you should not hesitate to express sympathy to someone in deep distress, even in a business environment. A colleague dealing with the fallout from a loved one's death, a child's severe illness, or a natural disaster that destroys their home—all of these and more merit your sympathy. But otherwise, remember that sympathy should be reserved for family, friends, or when your mission is to relieve emotional distress.

The key point is that empathy is at the core of the soft side of leadership, and it therefore deserves your attention. But there's another side to leadership that you also need to nurture and apply when necessary: the hard side.

THE HARD SIDE: BUSINESS ACUMEN

I have so far emphasized the soft side of leadership as you have already developed the hard skills of selling through your initial training and your practical experience. However, the transition to the 3rd sales transformation requires a greater mastery of hard skills which I refer to as *business acumen*.

There are many definitions of business acumen, but a simple one that I have personally used is the following: "Business acumen is the ability to readily comprehend how business value is created."

As you can see from this definition, we already have covered this at a strategic level in Chapter 4, where we explored mastering multiple objectives with the three drivers of profitability, market share, and customer satisfaction. This gave us the big picture of how a business makes money in the short, medium, and long term.

But at a very pragmatic level, business acumen means that you also need to be able to quickly understand the business implications of a decision. Speed is indeed an important component of business acumen. Dealing with a situation to deliver a good outcome requires not only financial agility, but also good reflexes. What I'm talking about is developing an intuition for what does (and does not) make good business sense. In other words, that's how you're street-smart when it comes to business issues. Let's illustrate this with a short example of how this applies to value capture and our quest for corporate-value creation.

In a meeting with Max, the buyer for a large industrial firm, you're pitching a specialized electric motor that the firm will use in its own products. The agreement with Max will involve three main aspects: price per unit, volume ordered, and an allowance. This allowance will cover free installation services as well as technical support for the first year. Whatever the buyer will use this allowance for, it will be deducted in calculating the profitability that your agreement will generate. You also know that in estimating the profitability of your sale, you should use a unit cost of $150 and this does not change with volume.

After a positive discussion with Max, you are at the point where you are confident you have a good appreciation of his needs, that you have convincingly demonstrated the value of the product to his firm, and that he is really interested in your product. This means that you have successfully completed the first selling phase and that you are now entering the second phase focused on negotiating the terms of an agreement. Based on all this, you make your first offer, which you know is on the high side and will not be accepted. But you feel that it is a good starting point for a negotiation. Here is your offer:

Price:	$200/unit
Volume:	10,000 units
Allowance:	$100,000

You have sales-support software on your tablet that will calculate the profitability of this potential agreement. But it would be better if you could swiftly make a mental estimate of this figure, as this would allow you to keep eye contact with Max and observe his facial and body language as you disclose this offer to him.

So, think fast—what is the profitability of this offer for your firm? And please do not read the next paragraph until you have your answer!

There are several ways to get to that number, but one path is to first find that your unit margin at this price is $50. You would then multiply the unit margin by the volume of 10,000 units to get a total margin of $500,000. Finally, you would subtract the allowance of $100,000 to get to a total profit of $400,000. Easy, right?

Now, you are in a better position to anticipate the next rounds of negotiations. For this, you will want to appreciate how the profitability of this agreement will be sensitive to different possible reactions from Max. You could again find the precise numbers using the sales-support software on your tablet, but you still want to keep eye contact with Max. So, it's better for you to make a quick guess for what would happen if Max responded by indicating that he needs only a volume of 8,000 units instead of 10,000 for the price and allowance that you proposed. Can you mentally estimate the drop in the profitability of the agreement in that case?

In the same way as before, you can quickly estimate that profit will decrease to $300,000. But what is important to realize is that a drop in volume of 20 percent (from 10,000 to 8,000 units) would result in a larger drop in profitability of 25 percent (from $400,000 to $300,000).

Another possibility you consider is that Max will ask for a better price. You wonder what it would imply for the profitability of the agreement if Max asked for a price reduction of 10 percent for the same volume and allowance.

The price reduction of 10 percent—to $180 a unit—would reduce the unit margin to $30. The profit would thus drop to $300,000 minus the allowance, resulting in a final profit of $200,000. You realize that the 10 percent cut in price would lead to a 50 percent drop in profitability, a dramatically sensitive outcome!

You now turn to a significant increase in allowance to impress Max of your desire to reach an agreement, while avoiding a cut in price or volume. What would happen to your profitability if you increased the allowance by 40 percent?

This is an easy one. Your allowance would increase by $40,000, so your profit would drop from $400,000 to $360,000. This means a reduction in profitability of only 10 percent for an increase in the allowance of 40 percent!

How did you do in your own responses to the above questions? If you did not take the time to do this speed maths, you can do it now by filling the blanks in Table 6.1, without, of course, looking at the answers above. If you can do it in less than 60 seconds, you are doing great; in less than 30 seconds you are exceptional. An effective and easy way to develop your mental agility for value capture is to repeat this type of fun exercises with different numbers.

Table 6.1   Mental agility for value capture.

	(%)	Volume (units)	Price ($)	Unit margin ($)	Allowance ($)	Profitability ($)
Base offer		10,000	200	50	100,000	400,000
Volume	-20	**8,000**	200	50	100,000	?
Price	-10	10,000	**180**	?	100,000	?
Allowance	+40	10,000	200	50	**140,000**	?

It's important to note that having business acumen doesn't mean you have to be exactly right with every answer, because being close is often good enough when you are making quick decisions. The aim is for you to have a good sense of how altering different elements of a contract will affect the business.

Now you know the very different sensitivities of profitability in the above example: highest for price, second for volume, lowest for the allowance. Of course, what you would need to explore further is how your counterpart, Max, the buyer, values these variations in each of your three negotiation variables. But knowing the sensitivity of your objective to the variables in a negotiation is the first step.

Having the mental agility to appreciate what affects your objective develops your business acumen and also develops the confidence you need to lead your way through a negotiation, while keeping your attention on your customer's reactions. This is essential for exploring the different options available within a contract and working out which one will deliver the best value for the corporation, as well as meeting the needs of the client.

The above example considered only one of the drivers of corporate-value creation, profitability. Indeed, financial aspects are those that come most to mind when discussing business acumen. However, as the expression indicates, it requires developing one's sensitivity to *all* business aspects of a particular situation, which is the creation of corporate value as you face this new challenge.

After considering these precepts on the soft and the hard side of leadership, let's now dig a bit deeper into how you can develop your own personal leadership attitude as a sales professional—and some of the obstacles you might encounter along the way.

Your Personal Growth as a Leader

Many people consider themselves to be employees of an organization, paid to perform a defined set of tasks. Improvements come by repeating these tasks over time, the so-called *experience effect*. When the situation evolves, or when new techniques or approaches become available, employees must learn to perform these tasks in different ways. When this occurs, their firm will initiate and organize training programmes to respond to this need,

Most firms today understand the value of investing in the personal development of their employees. For example, companies deploy all sorts of training programmes for their sales pros, most often to introduce new products or new selling techniques.

With the new focus on corporate-value creation, you as a sales professional may attend training programmes that address many of the same topics covered in this book. The point of this chapter, however, is to show that to win in the 3rd sales transformation, you need to take responsibility for your own continuous personal leadership development, beyond the training programmes offered by your firm.

The 3rd sales transformation has many implications for sales pros, but a major one is that—with a responsibility to participate in the creation of corporate value—you must adopt a leadership attitude that goes beyond just being an employee. This starts by leading yourself into higher performance by continuously developing your own capabilities. In addition to having the hunger for self-improvement, this means that you must take time to make it happen. This is easier said than done, since most people are too busy concentrating on their assigned tasks to take the time they need to develop their capabilities.

The best story I know to drive this point home in a memorable way is the "sharpening the saw" parable described by Stephen Covey in his classic book, *The 7 Habits of Highly Effective People*. It goes as follows:

> As you are taking a walk through the woods, you encounter a man who has been working hard for *hours* to saw down a big tree. He looks exhausted. After a moment of thought, you suggest to him that if he took a short break to sharpen his saw, his task would be much faster. His response? "I don't have time to sharpen the saw. I'm too busy sawing!"[8]

Most employees would indeed not take the initiative to learn to increase their performance until they are induced (or perhaps ordered) into training programmes by their management. Those with a leadership attitude are different. They make sure to find the time for their personal development and to "sharpen their saw" on their own initiative—not after being prodded into it by management. It is an investment in time, but this time is well recovered by increased future performance.

How do you sharpen your saw? You can start by reviewing from time to time the concepts covered in this book. For instance, you have probably already realized that your capabilities on the soft and hard sides of leadership described in this chapter can always be developed. But new avenues for personal growth will always appear and you should be on the lookout for valuable and stimulating ideas from new books, podcasts, blog posts, articles, and other information sources.[9]

You will always be able to find ways to develop yourself if you have the courage to take the first essential step. This means that you will decide for yourself how much time per week to allocate to this activity, schedule it, and never miss these meetings with your most important customer: *you*.

To help ensure you are continuously stimulated on your journey of personal growth, here are two additional bits of advice commonly given to business leaders that you could benefit from.

The first is to *encourage feedback* from others. This does not need to be formal nor repetitive. Just seek new insights when you feel that it is appropriate, and from people who have different backgrounds and perspectives from your own. Make sure that you show a positive interest in what the other person tells you, and that you express your gratitude for it, whatever the nature of the feedback. And remember that the more you are surprised by the feedback, the more valuable it is. Do not refute it, try to dig deeper into it.

The other bit of advice is to *find yourself a mentor* with whom you can share ideas or doubts and have frank and honest discussions. This mentor could be inside or outside your firm, but in any case, not in a position to evaluate you as this would restrict the openness of your exchanges. But it should be someone with whom you can have regular encounters and on whom you can rely when in need.

EGO AND LEADERSHIP

But before you think that everything in the leadership world is sweetness and light, I need to warn you about one of the biggest barriers to great leadership: *ego*.

In workshops, I like to ask participants who they see as strongest leaders they do not like. Then we list their names. Please take a moment to do the same. Think about some of the strongest leaders you know—personally, or maybe through the media—and do not like. Write down their names on a list.

In my workshops, I next ask participants to tell me what these strong, unlikeable leaders have in common. Invariably, the response is "an oversized ego!" Is that also the case with the people you included on your list?

Having a strong ego can be a double-edged sword. It is a key ingredient in having a strong leadership attitude—you must be self-confident and assertive in the face of uncertainty and opposition. A sales pro with a strong ego will be more likely to take risks, stand up for their convictions, and inspire others to follow their lead. However, when that strong ego gets too big, that's when problems begin.

Egocentricity is an excessive focus on yourself and your own needs and wants at the expense of the needs and wants of others. Egotistical people display a variety of negative symptoms, including arrogance, excessive self-importance, lack of interest in others, preoccupation with oneself, and much more. This is when ego becomes the enemy of good leadership.[10]

Leaders with an overgrown ego tend to overestimate their own capabilities while ignoring or minimizing the contributions of others, especially negative feedback. People with independent judgment avoid their company, so they tend to be surrounded by weak yea-sayers and end up having a distorted vision of reality.

You need a strong ego to operate autonomously, survive adversity, and take initiative—qualities that are in the fundamental nature of selling. But to be a good leader, you must be acutely aware of your ego and manage it. This is a more modern business version of the old aphorism, "know thyself." As the ancient Greek philosopher Socrates explained, you have to search deep within your inner self to understand your true motives, strengths, and limitations. Only in this way can you build a favourable future for yourself and for others.

This knowledge of one's inner self is indeed the start of the path to becoming a more effective and balanced leader. A number of tools have been developed for this purpose, including self-administered questionnaires or audits.[11] Many companies have also adopted some form of so-called 360° tools, through which an individual can obtain structured feedback based on anonymous inputs from colleagues, friends, or family members.

The results are sometimes astounding for the individual concerned, while those who know this individual are not surprised at all. This reveals the gap between the individual's perception of their own self and the reality lived by those surrounding them.

This gap between perception and reality is a barrier to effective leadership. Short of psychotherapy, personal coaching, meditation, or mindfulness exercises, there are simple tools available that you can use to get to know yourself better.[12] Here are, for example, three easy and fun tasks to better discover your inner strengths and weaknesses, which are particularly relevant in the context of sales:

- Identify the *activities* you are most passionate about and those which you avoid or procrastinate with
- Reflect on the *occasions* when you have really positive or really negative emotions
- Think of the type of *people* you enjoy being with and those whose company creates grief for you

The pragmatic investigation of how you respond in the context of these activities, occasions, and people should allow you to realize where you excel and to protect yourself from undesirable mishaps. Having this information is the firm foundation you need to start looking further into leadership.

YOUR CORPORATE-VALUE CAPTURE MISSION

The last three chapters were devoted to the key capabilities to help you win in the 3rd sales transformation: mastering multiple objectives, steering customer satisfaction, and developing a leadership attitude. With this strong base, it's time to get into the specifics of value-capture selling.

In the chapters that follow, we'll dive deep into the skills related to sales negotiations for corporate-value capture, including preparation, strategy, tactics, and closure. The ultimate goal is to set you on the way to becoming a value-capture champion.

CHAPTER 7

PREPARATION FOR VALUE CAPTURE

Tom and his colleagues at ELTRON had thoroughly enjoyed participating in the WAWS programme. They could now better appreciate the new focus on corporate-value creation, and they were also reassured concerning the impact on their compensation—an unknown that had understandably made them particularly anxious. Tom and his fellow sales pros at ELTRON looked forward to the enrichment of their role resulting from the broader corporate-value perspective.

Tom reviewed his notes from the WAWS programme which was composed of two modules. In the first module, he appreciated the progress made by the organization's sales function in improving its interfaces, both with customers and marketing. While he knew this already, he enjoyed the refresher and the discussion around the improvements. The rationale for going through another transformation focused on corporate-value creation was new to him and made sense. This transformation would involve moving from a single revenue objective to multiple objectives corresponding to the key drivers of corporate-value creation in the short, medium, and long term: profitability, market share, and customer satisfaction.

WAWS participants were told that the revised sales-incentive system would integrate these multiple objectives. During the programme, the instructor presented a new sales-support software application meant to help sales professionals master this new system. He emphasized that the transformation to creating corporate value represented an upgrade in the responsibilities of sales pros, who would be required to assume a greater leadership role going forward.[1]

The second module of the WAWS programme presented the implications for sales negotiations resulting from this transformation. It contained both a review of key negotiation principles—valid in all types of negotiations—and an introduction to new elements specific to the focus on corporate-value creation. This module was entitled *value capture* to emphasize the objective of these negotiations.

Tom knew, however, that it would take time to become more effective in this new approach—for starters, he would have to prepare for the sales negotiations in an entirely new way. This made him particularly anxious because he would soon face his first sales negotiation meeting since participating in the WAWS programme. The meeting was with MARINTEK, a large manufacturer of pleasure boats which was potentially a new customer.

Tom had succeeded in making contact with Alan Chapman in the engineering department of MARINTEK about a year earlier. Alan was interested in the E150, a new solar panel charge controller (SPCC) made by ELTRON. The E150 is part of a new generation of products that efficiently gather energy from solar panels and store it in batteries. It was designed for a broad range of applications, including pleasure boats. About half a dozen competitors were able to make similar products, each with their own specificities.

Alan had brought Tom to several meetings at MARINTEK so that he could present the E150 to his colleagues, and especially Pat Costa from the manufacturing department. After a series of internal tests and investigations, Alan and Pat had approved the E150 for adoption on the boats produced in the coming year. They especially liked its efficiency, its expected lifetime, and its Bluetooth connectivity that allowed remote monitoring with a smartphone. In their discussions, Pat mentioned to Tom that MARINTEK would probably need between 10,000 and 20,000 units of SPCCs, from three to five suppliers, for the next model year.

Just before the WAWS programme sessions began, Alan and Pat congratulated Tom for becoming an approved supplier for the E150. They also told him that they were not in a position to discuss volume, price, or other terms with him as this was under the responsibility of the procurement department. They organized a meeting for Tom with Sue Newton in the procurement department, scheduled for two months later. As they parted, Alan told Tom half-jokingly that Sue was a tough negotiator and that she had earned the internal nickname "the shark!"

As he thought about how he would prepare for this sales-negotiation meeting with Sue, Tom remembered the story that his colleague Jack volunteered during the WAWS programme.

Jack had been working in sales for a few years and closed many deals, but he had often relied on his charm and persuasive abilities to seal the deal. He recounted to Tom his experience with a prospective customer who had expressed a need for a large amount of electronics. He had been successful in his discussions with the IT department, getting ELTRON onto the short list of suppliers. Excited by the opportunity, Jack was looking forward to the meeting organized by Sam, a buyer in the procurement department, to discuss the details of the deal with her.

The day of the meeting arrived, and Jack woke up feeling confident and ready to close the deal. However, as he began to review the information about the customer and their needs, he realized that he had not done enough research. He didn't know much about the customer's financials, nor their procurement approach, and he was not sufficiently prepared on his pricing options for different quantities.

Feeling unprepared, Jack tried to bluff his way through the meeting with Sam, but she was savvy and destabilized him with pointed questions on different financial scenarios. Jack realized that Sam was a really good professional buyer. He was not coherent in his approach and contradicted himself on one occasion, having to back-pedal on an offer when he realized it was a mistake. Sam could tell that Jack wasn't fully prepared, and she began to doubt his credibility and expertise in the field. The meeting ended without a deal, and Sam decided to go with another supplier.

Tom knew one thing from this cautionary tale: he absolutely did not want to end up in the same situation with Sue as Jack had with Sam.

THE ART OF PREPARATION

While you may sometimes be able to bluff your way through a sales negotiation, your chances of success are much greater when you do your homework instead of making it up as you go. In Jack's case, not preparing adequately for the sales negotiation with Sam left him not just without a deal, but he was embarrassed, disappointed, and his reputation was tarnished. Not a good look for a sales pro!

As a sales professional, you know the importance of preparation. You know your products and services in details, you know your customers, you know how to maximize the perceived customer value, you master your selling techniques . . . and so on. All this is good for the first phase of the selling process which aims to create customer interest—a desire to buy and a high WTP, as we saw in Chapter 2. In this first phase, the consultative-selling interaction with a customer is like a conversation. It will usually be wide open, exploratory, social, and relaxed. And it can lead to several meetings with different people.

The second phase of the selling process, concerning the negotiation of the terms of a potential agreement, is a very different situation. It will be focused—usually with a single professional buyer who wants to stay in control of the discussion. It will also tend to be tense, with possible silences and breaks, but a minimum of casual talk. Moves and countermoves must be carefully considered as there is little space to recover from any misstep. Your preparation for this second phase of the selling process is thus even more critical than for the first one. It has to be deep and focused on value capture.

The objective of a specific value-capture preparation is not only to avoid Jack's fate, but also to significantly increase your chances of closing a deal that creates greater corporate value.

Preparation for value capture will first give you a good understanding of the scope of financial possibilities existing within the commercial guidelines for your company's product, service, or solution. This will give you more confidence and authority when you're in a negotiation with the customer.

In addition, preparation will allow you to gain some understanding of the customer's requirements, financial situation, and procurement practices. This can help you establish credibility and trust with the customer and can also demonstrate that you are genuinely interested in finding a solution that works for them.

Most important, value-capture preparation will help you anticipate the customer's negotiation strategies and tactics, which can allow you to develop a more effective negotiating strategy of you own. This can enable you to gain more-favourable terms, reduce price objections, and increase the chances of closing the deal.

All these advantages can help you close the deal more effectively and at better terms for your company—creating significant corporate value in the process.

Of course, sales professionals and other people of action sometimes don't have the patience to spend the time they should preparing for a negotiation. This is the obstacle that prevents them from achieving their negotiating goals.

In his excellent book, *Dare to Prepare*, Ronald M. Shapiro nailed down this issue.[2] According to Shapiro, these are the three most common excuses for not preparing in advance of a negotiation:

- I don't have time
- I've done this before
- I know how to do this

All too often, busy sales pros believe they don't have time to prepare—there are other things on their minds, other priorities, other pressing issues that need their immediate attention. They may even see preparation as the boring part of a negotiation, with the negotiation itself being the fun, exciting, and fulfilling part. This illusion of lack of time is aided by the strong belief that this is a situation they have successfully handled numerous times before—"I know how to do this." And then they are unpleasantly surprised when the outcome is not the one they hoped for.

If you were to look at a negotiation as a huge iceberg, you would see that preparation comprises the vast majority of the iceberg—hidden below the water's surface and invisible to someone casually sailing by. But just because you can't see it doesn't mean it's not important. It is in fact the most important part of a successful negotiation, and it's the part that can cause your negotiation to sink if you aren't careful.

According to Effective Negotiation Services (ENS), more than 80 percent of a negotiation's outcome is a result of the preparation you do before you start your negotiation. As the organization says on its website, "Failing to prepare systematically in the pre-negotiation time commonly ends up with you spending at least three times more time and money in the post-negotiation time 'fighting the fires' lit by poor preparation."

Most relevant for value capture is a quote from the ancient Chinese military general and philosopher Sun Tzu in his classic book, *The Art of War*: "Every battle is won before it is ever fought."[3]

I am certain you've got the message by now. Value-capture selling demands a kind of preparation that is different from customer-value selling and which has to be approached systematically.

THE NEGOTIATION SETTING

If you have read any books on the topic of negotiation, you have probably noticed that many of the examples they present are of wide-open situations in business, politics, sports, diplomacy, and other domains. One of the key points in these contexts is to generate and explore the universe of possibilities to avoid what is called a *zero-sum game*, a situation where what is won by one party is at the expense of the other.[4]

In the first phase of a sales meeting—customer-value selling—the objective is to increase the size of the pie (a win-win approach). As discussed in Chapter 2, this first phase is focused on creating the maximum *perceived customer value* for the proposed offer, product, or service. In addition to creating interest and a desire to buy, the objective of this phase is to create a high WTP—willingness to pay—for the customer. This WTP is the size of the pie, the value to be shared between seller and buyer in the second phase of selling.

Negotiating for corporate value—the second phase of a sales meeting—is by nature a zero-sum game because the value the buyer captures from you is not available for your firm. The customer value of the offer will have to be shared between the supplier (price obtained) and the customer (WTP minus price paid). At this point, both buyer and seller are engaged in *value capture*.

The real negotiation starts in this second phase where you try to achieve an agreement with a high corporate value for your firm. This is where you want to make sure that you will get the biggest possible share of the pie for your firm. While you will always be negotiating with this goal in mind, be aware that you must also provide significant perceived value to your customer—the share of the pie that the customer will keep minus the price paid. Otherwise, why should they buy from you and not from some other firm?

These two phases of the selling process are not identified clearly in most books on sales negotiations, which explains the confusion sales pros often have when they are told about the value of win-win negotiations and end up in a zero-sum game. This book clearly focuses on the *second* phase of a sales encounter, the capture of value by each side—seller and buyer.

Every negotiation contains a desired *outcome* (the element that you try to obtain or maximize from the agreement) and *variables* (the elements that you can vary, and when they are determined, make an agreement).

The desired outcome we are focusing on is maximizing the corporate value from an agreement. As you'll recall from our previous discussions, we will consider that corporate value is determined by these three key drivers: profitability, market share, and customer satisfaction. Different firms can select other drivers for corporate value, without any loss in the applicability of the tools that we will explore. To keep this front of mind for you, the sales pro, your firm will align your own objectives (e.g., maximizing your bonus, building your reputation, and so on) with your company's objective to create corporate value. This is typically accomplished by linking your bonus to these three key drivers by way of a formula communicated to you and available in your sales-support application software.

In Chapter 6, we introduced three variables for a typical sales negotiation: price, volume, and an allowance. Again, in specific sales negotiations, the number of variables involved can be much larger and include such things as payment terms, detailed product specifications, services included, delivery conditions, agreement time span, and other elements. Limiting ourselves to three variables is simpler and is not limitative, the third element "allowance" including all other elements in addition to the main ones that are most often price and volume.[5]

We will thus consider in our examples the setting of the following sales negotiation: finding an agreement with a buyer on the variables of price, volume, and allowance to obtain the highest corporate value (as determined by the three drivers of profitability, market share, and customer satisfaction) for our firm.

With this negotiation setting in mind, let's look at the various aspects of how you can most effectively prepare for a sales negotiation.

PRIMARY PREPARATION

Most every book you read or course you take on negotiation will devote some space—usually a lot—to the important topic of preparation. Why? Because, as we have seen, preparation is key to negotiation success.

You may be familiar with the Program on Negotiation (PON) at the Harvard Law School. Founded in 1983, the programme has grown into one of the most-renowned centres for negotiation in the world. PON is the successor to the Harvard Negotiation Project, founded by Professor Roger Fisher, coauthor of the book, *Getting to Yes*—which set the bar high for books on the theory and practice of negotiation.

According to PON, failure to thoroughly prepare is the biggest mistake made by negotiators, and it is also a very common one. To help people avoid making this mistake, PON offers a 32-point pre-negotiation preparation checklist for negotiations of all kinds. While it is possible to break down the steps involved with negotiation preparation in many ways, I suggest that for sales professionals, preparing for a negotiation is a continuous process with two main stages:

Primary preparation. This takes place before a sales encounter and includes gathering and interpreting the facts and setting the scope of the negotiation. This stage includes investigating your negotiation possibilities and determining your lowest acceptable agreement.

Strategy preparation. This is the second stage of preparation before the sales encounter, and it centres on setting the broad lines that will guide your negotiation tactics to reach your goal. This includes anticipating the buyer's objectives and constraints.

These two stages of preparation should help you anticipate options for your sales negotiations, knowing that *during* the sales encounter you will have to continuously adapt your moves on the spot as you obtain more information from your counterpart. This includes developing a feeling for the customer's WTP, probing the buyer for their options, adjusting your strategy on the fly, adapting your tactics to the buyer's countermoves, and more.

The advantage of the primary and strategy preparation stages is that since they occur before your sales encounter, you can reflect on them calmly and not in the heat of the negotiation. In contrast, during the negotiation, you will have to think on your feet, which puts you under greater pressure. Clearly, the better prepared you are in advance of the negotiation, the better you can expect to do.

The rest of this chapter focuses on the first phase: primary preparation. Strategy preparation is the subject of Chapter 8 and live negotiation is discussed as part of Chapter 9, which focuses on tactics for value capture.

When you engage in primary preparation, you will need to gather and assess the following facts:

- Your target customer
- Your negotiating skills
- Your offer
- Your mission

Let's consider each of these aspects of primary preparation in turn.

UNDERSTANDING YOUR TARGET CUSTOMER

A negotiation is a battle of the minds, so it's critically important to know who you will be facing on the other side of the table. Note that your customer is both the business organization that is buying your products and services, *and* the person or people within the organization with whom you negotiate the deal. Both are important.

In the case of organizations, like snowflakes, each is different. Organizations have their own unique sets of practices, values, cultures, and more that differentiate them from one another. This is true even within an industry. Take, for example, retail. As you can imagine, Amazon and Walmart are very different organizations even though they sell many of the same things.

If you are a leader at Amazon, you are expected to adhere to the company's 16 leadership principles, which include such things as "think big," "dive deep," and "bias for action." If you're a leader at Walmart, you may be expected to lead your people in the Walmart Cheer after employee meetings that start a shift. And as you can imagine, Apple and IBM are very different organizations, as are Tesla and General Motors.

The point is that you need to fully comprehend your target customer—their culture, practices, what they value, and so on—*before* you enter into a sales negotiation with them, not after. You can do this in a variety of ways, including:

- Reviewing social media accounts such as LinkedIn, Instagram, and Twitter
- Contacting colleagues, friends, and others who have negotiated with or know the individual
- Making a personal preliminary call with the individual to casually get to know the person and learn more about their perspectives before the first actual negotiation encounter

Most important in negotiations are precedents that can frame expectations in the mind of your target customer. This includes any previous negotiations with your firm and the agreements that resulted from them, along with any previous negotiations and agreements of this target customer with other suppliers. You might also be able to find articles and stories about other negotiations and agreements in news media or association newsletters.

Keep in mind that it's impossible to have perfect knowledge about your target customer because of the richness of both organizations and individuals, and the simple fact that your research time is going to be constrained (you need to devote time to other selling tasks, after all!). But taking the time to create a base of knowledge on the organization and the person you'll be negotiating with will build your self-confidence, provide you with prompts for a fruitful discussion, and give you more chances for a better negotiation outcome.

MASTERING YOUR NEGOTIATING SKILLS

While we will look at the process of negotiation strategy and tactics in detail in the next two chapters, what you should be aware of in your primary preparation are your own negotiating skills and your strengths and weaknesses as a negotiator. Your emotional control and empathy are crucial in negotiations, and they echo our discussions of these topics in terms of leadership attitude in Chapter 6.

As you assess your negotiation skills, you should also be particularly aware of how you rate yourself on the following:

Verbal and nonverbal communication. This includes expressing yourself clearly, listening actively to the other party, decrypting the subtle verbal and nonverbal messages being sent to you, and sending your own low-key signals in return.

The art of asking questions. Good questions are an effective way to show interest in the other party and to gather valuable information.

Patience and silence management. Many action-oriented people are impatient and embarrassed by silence. They feel the need to talk just to fill a silent space. This is not effective in negotiations and can in fact be counterproductive. So, it's important to learn to be more patient and to cope with long periods of silence, inducing the other party to communicate information more often and more completely.

Assertiveness. When you are in a selling position, you want to show that you are at the service of your buyer, and you would like to have their business. This does not mean that you should accept any and all of their requests and never say no. Assertiveness is the crucial skill in negotiations that enables you to speak up directly for your interests, while showing respect for the other parties and their positions.

Adaptability. New information is likely to crop up in negotiations, perhaps when you least expect it. Good preparation helps you react appropriately to such contingencies, but you will still need to have a high level of adaptability to succeed. This requires remaining calm, keeping an open mind, and taking the time to reflect for effective responses.

The most useful tool for improving your negotiating skills is to debrief yourself after each sales encounter. Where have you particularly excelled? Where could you have done better? What have you learned to increase your negotiation capabilities? The debrief does not need to be long or take up hours of your time. Bullet points are particularly effective, and you can set aside just 10 or 15 minutes to complete the task. But to be of any value, it should be written and easily accessible.

Grasping Your Offer

For the first phase of the selling process, you needed to master the specifications of your firm's products or services, all of which contribute to the creation of a high perceived value by the customer.

In the second phase of the sales process, with its focus on corporate-value creation, commercial guidelines are most important as they determine the variables that can be used in the negotiation process. These guidelines will usually include such things as:

- List price up to a certain volume
- Discount structure with a maximum discount for different volume levels
- Additional discount at the discretion of the sales pro
- Maximum allowance given as an absolute number or as a percentage of the order

To illustrate these specific aspects of primary preparation, let's go back to our super sales pro Tom at ELTRON, preparing his offer for Sue, the professional buyer at MARINTEK. Tom must carefully consider the commercial guidelines handed down to him by his management at ELTRON for the E150, as indicated in Table 7.1.

This is the kind of preparation required to grasp your offer before you enter a sales negotiation. Your organization's commercial guidelines determine the universe of options you have available for your negotiations. If you have a sales-support application, it will help you explore these options. But in any case, it's always a good idea to mentally prepare yourself in advance for the realm of possibilities available.

Table 7.1　Commercial guidelines for the E150 model.

Costs and allowances	Conditions for price and units	Restrictions on use
List price	$300/unit up to 2,000 units	Public information known to customers
Maximum discount	$15 for every extra 1,000 units above 2,000	Not to be communicated to customers
Maximum additional discount	$1/unit for every extra 1,000 units above 2,000	To be used exceptionally, at the discretion of sales pros
Maximum allowance	8 percent of the order	To be used only at the customer's request or to close a deal
Minimum price allowed	$140/unit	No quantity discount below this level
Unit cost	$100/unit	To be used to estimate profitability of a contract

FOCUSING ON YOUR VALUE-CAPTURE MISSION

When preparing for your sales encounter, you need to have a clear understanding of your mission and focus on it: maximizing the corporate value created by your sales negotiation. This requires always keeping in mind the three key drivers of corporate value: profitability, market share, and customer satisfaction.

You need to know how this mission is expressed in terms of these drivers of corporate value. Tom's value-capture mission for the MARINTEK account has been clearly expressed in terms of these objectives.[6]

- **Profitability: $500,000.** Tom has been told this is a lower-than-expected profitability objective relative to the size of MARINTEK, but his firm has decided to make a significant financial concession to gain this major customer.

- **Market share:** 60 percent. This would make ELTRON, Tom's firm, the primary supplier for MARINTEK, which has gained a major position in its sector. It is expected that the customer wants to source its solar panel charge controllers from three suppliers.
- **Customer satisfaction:** 70 percent. Tom's management wants to build a long-term relationship with MARINTEK and estimates that this is a proper objective for that purpose.

Looking at these objectives, Tom realizes that they are more complex than the simple revenue target he has received in the past. But because of his participation in the WAWS programme, Tom now understands their rationale and how to use them. Price and volume are indeed the key variables, with a high sensitivity on corporate value, and the allowance is the "oil" that can make a deal go through with a lesser negative impact on corporate value.

Regardless, Tom is still somewhat anxious because he will have to adopt a different approach than he is used to. Previously, he would have listened carefully to the customer's needs, identified their price expectations, negotiated hard to contain their requirements, and in the end accepted their final "last counteroffer" to make the sale. Now he sees that he is more constrained and has additional chances to lose the sale. He appreciates that this is to avoid a deal that would destroy corporate value, and agrees with this mission, but sees that it is going to be a more challenging type of sales negotiation.

As he reviews how best to achieve his objectives, Tom realizes that he will be able to easily calculate the profitability of an offer with the sales-support software application on his tablet. Calculating the market share corresponding to an offer is also easy. The result is actually close to the revenues he was trying to maximize using the old approach, except it is now relative to the buyer's annual need. This information should not be too difficult to obtain from the buyer and in any case is quite useful.

Tom also knows that the customer-satisfaction rating will be obtained through a special service that will contact the buyer within two weeks after the concluded call. He realizes, however, that he must be sensitive to the buyer's reactions during the sales negotiation to continuously evaluate and manage her satisfaction with the encounter and the agreement obtained. In this way, Tom can avoid any unpleasant surprises when he receives the buyer's satisfaction rating.

With a clear understanding of his commercial guidelines and of his value-capture mission, Tom goes back to his WAWS notes concerning the next stage of his primary preparation: Setting your BATNA.

Do You Know Your BATNA?

Now that you have gathered all the elements for your negotiation, you need to have a clear view of the lowest deal you are ready to accept. In their classic book on the topic of negotiation, *Getting to Yes*,[7] Roger Fisher and William Ury introduced the world to BATNA, which stands for "Best Alternative To a Negotiated Agreement"—the very best outcome you can expect to attain elsewhere if you fail to reach an agreement in your negotiation. In the years since their book was originally published in 1981, BATNA has taken the world by storm, becoming the most-diffused negotiation concept ever.

Knowing your BATNA is useful in a negotiation because it helps you determine your minimum acceptable outcome. It provides a benchmark for evaluating any proposed agreement and helps ensure that you do not accept a deal that is worse than your next-best alternative. Having a clear BATNA in mind can help you avoid making concessions that are not in line with your interests, and to walk away from a negotiation that is not favourable to you. You won't be tempted to accept a deal that you should have rejected, just to reach an agreement—*any* agreement.

Let's start with a classic simple example before applying BATNA in a B2B context. You've decided it's time to sell your house. It was a great house to raise your kids in, with plenty of room and a big backyard. But now that your children have moved out and started their own families, you and your spouse don't need all that room anymore. So, in preparation for your sales negotiations, you'll set both a base (asking) price for your home and a BATNA—the lowest amount below which you'll reject any offers you receive.

Keep in mind that your BATNA can include a variety of elements besides the price. In the case of selling a home, for example, you might also consider whether the buyer is paying cash or must get bank approval for a mortgage loan, how quickly they are willing to close the deal, if they are willing to waive an inspection of the premises, whether they will lease back the home to you for a certain period of time while you search for your next home, and so on. However, for this example, we'll focus solely on price.

When determining both your base price and your BATNA, you'll survey the local market of homes in your area, seeking recent sales of similar properties. Let's say, for example, that your home is 3,000 square feet in size, it's on a 1-acre lot next to a lake, and the home was built 50 years ago. While most homes of that vintage are showing their age, yours was renovated to a high standard just two years ago.

So, to set your base price and BATNA, you find through public records the prices for similar homes—close to the same size, on a lot that's about the same size and type, and in about the same condition as yours—that sold within the past six months to a year. If you can't find exact or even close matches, you can extrapolate numbers to suit your needs.

After reviewing the comps, you decide on a base price of $400,000 and a BATNA of $350,000. The base price is on the high side of the comps, and you and your spouse will celebrate with a bottle of champagne if you achieve it. Figure 7.1 shows the BATNA for your home, the base price, and the negotiating range in between.

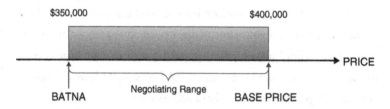

Figure 7.1   The home seller's BATNA.

Anything below your BATNA will cause you to automatically reject the offer and save the champagne for another occasion. So, you will work hard to obtain offers that are above your BATNA and then vigorously negotiate them to get as close to your base price as you can.

You might, for example, hire a top-notch real estate broker to represent you and to push the deal price higher in the sales negotiation. Or you might clean your house from top to bottom and make some minor repairs to ensure buyers are impressed by what they see—hopefully offering more money for your home.

One thing to keep in mind is that your BATNA may evolve depending on the specifics of your situation. If the home sits on the market with no offers for several months, or if you suddenly need the cash from the sale of your home to finance a new business venture, you may decide to lower your BATNA in a bid to accelerate the sales process and reach a deal with a buyer. BATNAs are situational, and subject to the seller's wants and needs at any particular time.

The BATNA Frontier for Value Capture

In a B2B sales situation, the BATNA is defined by commercial guidelines (e.g., list price, maximum discount, etc.), which we explored in the "Grasping Your Offer" section above.

Let's go back to Tom, who is preparing for his upcoming sales negotiation with Sue. Given the 10,000–20,000 units range that Pat mentioned as the volume needed for MARINTEK's needs, Tom decided to first consider 10,000 units as a possible target. This would correspond to 67 percent of the 15,000-unit midrange indicated by Pat, above his market share objective of 60 percent. The list price for the E150 is set at $300/unit up to 2,000 units with a maximum discount of $15 for every 1,000 units above 2,000.

For a volume of 10,000 units, the maximum quantity discount is thus $120/unit ($15 x 8), giving a price of $180/unit at maximum discount. Adding the additional discretionary discount of $1 for every 1,000 units above 2,000, the BATNA is $172/unit. This gives a negotiating range of $172 to $300, as shown in Figure 7.2.

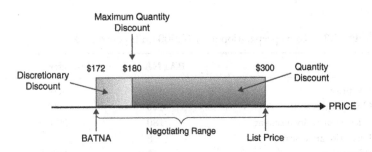

Figure 7.2   The sales pro's BATNA.

Tom then looked at the implications of different offers he could make when starting the negotiation with Sue. He reached the conclusion that $200/unit could be a good first offer. With a unit cost of $100/unit, this would result in a profit of $1,000,000—double his objective. At this point, Tom did not find it useful to look at the impact of an allowance on profitability as he planned to use it as a concession only at a late stage in the negotiations. While he could not anticipate Sue's satisfaction with such an offer, Tom used his sales-support application to evaluate the corporate value that it would generate, just based on this profitability and the estimated market share of 67 percent for 10,000 units. The corporate value created by this offer was 142 percent of the mission given to him compared with 120 percent at his BATNA, assuming that Sue was also satisfied with the result (see Table 7.2, for a comparison of Tom's BATNA with his first considered offer). Tom observed that a first offer of $200/unit for a volume of 10,000 units well exceeded both his profitability and market-share objectives and generated a substantial corporate value. It also gave him considerable space to make concessions during the negotiations.

Table 7.2   Tom's preparation for a 10,000 units contract ($).

	BATNA	First offer
List price	300	300
Quantity discount	120	100
Price on quantity discount	180	200
Discretionary discount	8	0
Price offered	172	200
Profitability	720,000	1,000,000
Corporate value as % of objective	120	142

Tom appreciates, however, that at this point in time he does not precisely know Sue's exact needs. He realizes that he may have been very ambitious in planning for the opening of his negotiation with a volume as high as 10,000 units. As the negotiation proceeds, Tom also understands that he will have to readily investigate different volume and price combinations. Knowledge of a single BATNA at $172 is not sufficient in a situation when the negotiation is likely to cover a volume range. Tom thus proceeded to determine his BATNA for different volume levels from the minimum order of 2,000 units to what he expected was a maximum acceptable limit for MARINTEK at 16,000 units. This gave Tom a BATNA frontier,[8] as shown in Figure 7.3.

This BATNA frontier shows the minimum acceptable price for different volume levels. Any combination above this line is acceptable for ELTRON, and so the purpose of the negotiation will be to

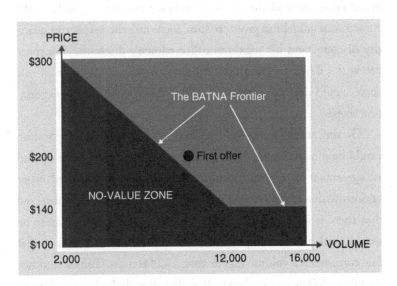

Figure 7.3   The sales pro's BATNA frontier.

obtain an agreement above that line that maximizes corporate value while also being acceptable to Sue and MARINTEK.

Note that this particular BATNA frontier is based on only the two most important variables of a negotiation: price and volume. Where are the other variables of the negotiation that are combined in what we called "allowance?" As the targeted outcome of corporate value is less sensitive to these other elements (see the representative example in Chapter 4), they are used to provide concessions in the negotiation. We will dig deeper into the art of making concessions in Chapter 9 on value-capture tactics. This will be used to obtain an agreement that is both as favourable as possible, and as high as possible above the BATNA frontier.

Tom used his sales-support software to investigate his BATNA for different volume levels and to be better prepared for his negotiation with Sue. Note that the BATNA frontier in Figure 7.3 gives the broad perspective of the negotiation space that corresponds to the commercial guidelines given to Tom, including the maximum quantity discount and his maximum discretionary discount. The space below the BATNA frontier is the *no-value zone*. Any price in this space would destroy corporate value and is outside of the negotiation scope.

Getting stuck on one volume level in one's strategy preparation would be a mistake, and Tom realizes that if he is not able to find an agreement as a primary supplier, he could move toward other options with a lower volume but higher price. He has also observed that there is an inflection point at around 12,000 units where he would reach the lowest price allowed of $140. This means that if Sue considered a volume higher than 12,000 units, Tom would not be able to follow in her demands if they already had come close to that level.

The clear understanding of one's BATNA frontier is the final stage of the primary preparation for value capture. It is of course undisclosed by the sales pro and unknown to the buyer.

Tom must now combine his own BATNA frontier with the expectations he has for Sue's BATNA frontier. And this coming battle of the minds between Tom and Sue requires further preparation on Tom's part. The focus of this further preparation will be his strategy for value capture—the topic of Chapter 8. As you can well imagine, the strategy Tom decides on will have a major impact on the success—or failure—of his sales negotiation.

CHAPTER 8

VALUE-CAPTURE STRATEGY

Let's revisit our sales pro, Tom. As he reflects on his primary preparation, he realizes that he needs to further prepare for his meeting with Sue, the buyer for his prospective customer, MARINTEK. In particular, he will have to anticipate a variety of different options according to Sue's needs and negotiation approach as well as her firm's desire to maximize corporate value—all while Tom works hard to maximize his own bonus.

A complicated formula, with many moving parts!

So, before actively preparing his negotiation strategy, Tom decided it was a good time to review his notes from the WAWS programme. He was glad that he had taken plenty of notes because they would be very helpful for gaining a better understanding of what value-capture strategy is all about and what an appropriate approach would be before going into his meeting with Sue. And, as it turned out, he was right on both counts.

In business, we hear a lot about strategy, but it's not always so clear what strategy is. When it comes to value-capture selling, strategy is about setting the broad lines that will allow you to reach your goal, which is to maximize the corporate value from a negotiation. To succeed, you need to devote time and focus and energy to creating your strategy.

A frequent source of failure is to jump too quickly into deciding a strategy—before you survey the entire environment in which you will negotiate your deal. Strategy cannot be effective unless it has been preceded by some solid homework, like the preliminary preparation described in Chapter 7. As Benjamin Franklin once warned, "By failing to prepare, you are preparing to fail."[1]

Another source of failure is mistakenly thinking that strategy is a detailed plan of action, setting forth every step you'll take along the way. This is not the case at all. Strategy is not a detailed plan of action; it is a mental image.[2] Its purpose is to provide direction to guide the tactics that you will deploy during the negotiation, as we will see in Chapter 9. Formulating a strategy is thus the last phase of preparation before you enter the sales negotiation with a buyer.

When you strategize ahead of any negotiation, it is vital that you are realistic about the potential outcomes. There are four possible outcomes to any negotiation, in decreasing order of desirability for you the sales professional:

- Agreement in favour of the seller
- Balanced agreement
- Agreement in favour of the buyer
- No agreement

An agreement in your favour is the most desirable outcome. Note that with your goal of maximizing corporate value, the quality of this outcome is based on the three key drivers of corporate value: profitability, market share, and customer satisfaction. Also note that an "agreement in favour of the seller" (you) means that you captured a high corporate value and does *not* mean that you acted to the detriment of the buyer.

If, for example, you were able to squeeze from a buyer a deal with a high profitability for your company, ending up with increased market share but also a dissatisfied customer, you would probably be penalized with a lower corporate value and consequently a lower bonus. An agreement in your favour means that you will have done well on all three objectives driving corporate value—*including* customer satisfaction.

A balanced agreement is less preferable than an agreement in your favour. When you negotiate a balanced agreement, the customer's satisfaction will likely be high, but your company will end up with lower levels of profitability and market share. Therefore, the corporate value you captured is less than it could potentially be.

An agreement in favour of the buyer means that the profitability of the agreement could likely have been higher for you. And while the buyer will have very high satisfaction by "winning" the sales negotiation—which contributes to the corporate value of this agreement for your firm—they may want to buy everything they can from you. This outcome will maximize your market share, but corporate value will suffer because of the reduced profitability. Again, your bonus will be reduced or perhaps even wiped out entirely.

No agreement is, of course, the worst outcome from a negotiation—not just for you, but also for your customer. When there is no agreement, you walk away with nothing, and corporate value does not increase. It may, in fact, decrease because the customer may be so angry with you that they may not consider you as a viable supplier in the future. And no agreement is also bad for your customer because they didn't get the products or services they need. They'll now have to seek out other suppliers. Note, however, that you can always derive a benefit from a failed customer negotiation—the lessons learned that you will be able to use in future sales negotiations.

I'm sure you've heard the oft-quoted saying, "better a bad agreement than no agreement at all." This rationale has traditionally been used to justify making deep price cuts to generate revenues, often resulting in the destruction of corporate value for the firm. With a focus on creating corporate value, the commercial guidelines should stop you from negotiating a deal that destroys corporate value. This is what setting your BATNA, as discussed in Chapter 7, protects you from.

So, the bad agreement that is still better than no agreement at all is the agreement in favour of the buyer but above your BATNA. Not as good as the first two, but definitely better than no agreement at all.

The Buyer's BATNA

In the same way that you try to maximize your corporate value outcome in any sales negotiation, the buyers you face across the table have their own goals they must try to achieve and constraints they must work within. And it's likely that you will run up against those goals and constraints as you proceed in your negotiation.

Let's return to our example of house selling, where you had set a price of $400,000 but were willing to accept an offer as low as $350,000. Do you remember why we first looked at this example? Because it's the simplest possible example, and a good principle is to master the simplest example before taking on one that is more complex. And why is this the simplest example? Because there is only one negotiation variable, price, and the outcome is the same as this variable, price.

Now, let's try to put ourselves in the shoes of a potential buyer, Ms. Morgan Snow.

Ms. Snow is looking to buy a house, ideally for around $320,000, because that is the maximum amount she can personally raise, including the mortgage approved by her banker. She saw an ad for your house, but the published price of $400,000 is significantly higher than what she can afford. However, Ms. Snow really likes what she saw in the ad, and she sees herself living happily with her family in the house. So, she refuses to give up trying to buy it.

First, Ms. Snow knows that your listed price is on the high end of what you expect to get—the price per square foot is a bit higher than that for comparable homes currently for sale. Second, she knows that she can gather some cash from her family, up to $50,000. The maximum price she could afford to pay is thus $370,000. She really cannot go above this limit and is furthermore convinced that for this price she is sure to find a very satisfying home. This is consequently Ms. Snow's BATNA, the *best alternative to a negotiated agreement*. It is the same idea as for you the seller, except Snow's BATNA as the buyer is an upper limit as shown in Figure 8.1, while your BATNA is a lower limit.

Morgan Snow knows that she would regret it forever if she did not make the effort to buy your house despite the price gap, and she's hopeful you will be willing to reduce your price in pursuit of a deal. She therefore contacts you to set up an appointment for a showing. If she still likes what she sees, she plans to immediately make you a formal offer to buy it—at a price she can afford.

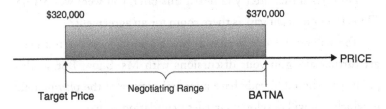

Figure 8.1   The home buyer's BATNA.

Obviously, the only information available to both you and the buyer is the published price of $400,000. You do not know Ms. Snow's financial situation—her banker's upper limit on a mortgage loan, and the money she can borrow from family members—and Ms. Snow does not know if or how far you would be willing to drop your price in pursuit of a deal. But as you prepare for a possible negotiation, you can anticipate that if Ms. Snow really likes your house, she can improve her offer up to a certain point of resistance—her explicit or implicit BATNA.

Do You Know ZOPA?

The next day, Morgan Snow arrives at the appointed time to see for herself if your house is as wonderful as she thinks it is. During the showing, you have an opportunity to point out all the great features of your home—the large lot size next to a lake, the recent interior renovation, the quality of the neighbourhood, and how perfect the home was for you to raise your own family. After the showing, Ms. Snow confirms her interest and decides to make an offer to purchase your house.

She knows that you want to sell your house for $400,000—the advertised price—but she cannot afford it. Ms. Snow therefore offers just $320,000. "I completed an exhaustive review of the comps for similar homes in the area," she tells you, "and my offer is a fair one."

I'm certain that after you heard this offer, you were wondering, "This is a significant gap, is there room for an agreement?"

You will not be able to answer this question, however, until you get further along in your discussions with Ms. Snow. But, at this point, you should already have a mental picture of the playing field in which you will develop your sales negotiation strategy.

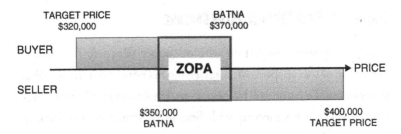

Figure 8.2   The home negotiation ZOPA.

If you could combine both your own view of this negotiation, along with Ms. Snow's, you could determine if there is a ZOPA—a *zone of potential agreement*.[3] As shown in Figure 8.2, such a zone indeed exists between $350,000 and $370,000.

However, neither of you has this information—you are in the dark. It could be that Ms. Snow is bluffing in sharing her target price, and that she can actually afford to meet your asking price. In this case, the ZOPA is wide and covers all your own range of possibilities between your target price and your BATNA.

You can imagine how the negotiation tactics will be different if the ZOPA is narrow or if it is broad.

But it could also be that Ms. Snow cannot gather more than $340,000, in which case there is no ZOPA. Even with all the possible goodwill and motivation on both sides to make a deal, no agreement will be possible. That is, of course, unless you lower your BATNA. But if that turns out to be the case, it means that $350,000 was not your true BATNA—your true BATNA was something lower. How low are you really willing to go?

This is the acid test on the quality of your preparation. Your BATNA should give you the confidence required for your negotiation, and it has to be the absolute rock bottom of what you are ready to accept, whatever the persuasive arguments the other party may make.

Visualizing Your ZOPA for Value Capture

Let's pick up where we left off with our super sales pro, Tom, at the beginning of this chapter. After reviewing his notes from the WAWS programme, Tom ponders his next steps. He knows that he must prepare further for his meeting with Sue. In particular, he will have to anticipate different options according to her needs and negotiation approach, along with his firm's desire to maximize corporate value. Tom already knows that Sue's firm, MARINTEK, appreciates the value of the E150, as Alan from engineering and Pat from manufacturing were impressed by it and approved ELTRON as a supplier. Sue will thus be concerned only about the terms of an agreement.

Tom starts by keeping his reasoning simple—a first possible offer at just one level of volume. Reminding himself of his primary preparation, he knows that with a list price of $300/unit and a volume of 10,000 units, his BATNA is $172/unit, taking into account the maximum volume discount as well as his additional discretionary discount.

Tom knows that Sue is a professional buyer who has likely attended numerous procurement training courses over the years and has perhaps gained some professional certifications as a result. In addition, she likely has clear purchasing guidelines from MARINTEK's management, with expectations for quantity discounts and allowances based on order size.

Sue meets many sales pros like Tom, competing against Tom's firm or selling other types of products and services, and she has done her homework. Her firm has a requirement for a target volume of SPCCs that she can fulfill with a single supplier, or spread across several suppliers. Her mission is to secure this volume at the lowest possible total cost, and she is incentivized on this objective. She has a good understanding of the market and of the range of prices that she can expect from several suppliers. She knows all about BATNAs and has defined one for this purchase. Sue also assumes that Tom knows his own BATNA.

Based on his discussions with Alan and Pat, Tom knew that Sue needs to secure up to 20,000 units of the solar panel charge controllers, and estimated that her actual sourcing plan was for around 16,000 units. As a first guess, he thought that she would prefer to buy up to a volume of 10,000 units from a primary supplier, and the remaining volume from two or three other suppliers to provide her with security of sourcing and bargaining power. Tom figured that at a volume of 10,000 units, her target price could be as low as $150 and her BATNA could be as high as $200. This, of course, is Tom's best guess at this particular time, and its accuracy would be tested during the negotiation.

Given this best guess, Tom draws the following visualization of the negotiation space for an order of 10,000 units (Figure 8.3).

Tom realizes that this is only his visualization of the ZOPA and that the reality on Sue's side could be quite different. Regardless, he is fully confident in his side of the picture, as he should be, including the list price and his BATNA, which come from his firm's commercial guidelines. The uncertainty obviously comes from his estimates

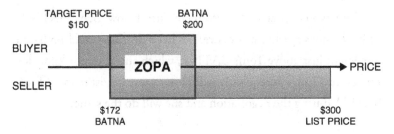

Figure 8.3   The sales negotiation ZOPA.

of Sue's desired purchase quantity, and her target price and BATNA. But Tom feels that this is his best estimate, given the information he has been able to gather during his primary preparation.

Tom also anticipates that, as a professional buyer, Sue has made a similar analysis. She is probably fully confident of her own target price and BATNA, and she is aware of Tom's list price. But she obviously does not know Tom's BATNA for 10,000 units, and she has made her own estimate, which may be different than Tom's $172.

AIMING FOR AN AGREEMENT

Tom feels that in the first stage of his negotiation with Sue, he should aim to become her primary supplier with a volume of 10,000 units. Any agreement to be reached will have to be in the ZOPA that he has identified, assuming his assumptions are correct.

Tom now visualizes the three positive outcomes that he reviewed at the beginning of this chapter (Figure 8.4):

- An agreement to his advantage would be toward the high end of the ZOPA
- A balanced agreement would be toward the middle of the ZOPA
- An agreement to Sue's advantage would be toward the bottom end of the ZOPA

Tom would prefer an agreement just below Sue's BATNA, which he does not know for sure. On her side, Sue would prefer an agreement just above Tom's BATNA, which she does not know for sure either. Tom consequently will have to test his estimate of Sue's BATNA during the negotiation and she will do the same.

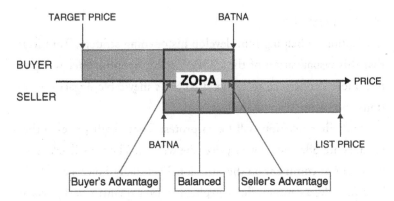

Figure 8.4   The three positive outcomes.

Tom remembers from WAWS that the first offer he makes is particularly important in value-capture tactics, and this visualization of the ZOPA should also give him more confidence for his opening offer.

Given his appraisal of the ZOPA, a strategy to make a first offer for a volume of 10,000 units at a price of $210/unit, just above Sue's expected BATNA, seems appropriate to Tom. If his estimation of Sue's BATNA is correct, he knows that she will certainly not accept this offer. But he also knows that, as a professional buyer, she would never accept his first offer anyway, whatever it may be.

Starting above the ZOPA gives Tom plenty of room to manoeuvre his price down, without neglecting the possibility of also using the allowance that he has available to offer. In addition, Tom remembers from his WAWS session on customer satisfaction that Sue will derive a higher level of satisfaction when she wins a price discount after a tough negotiation.[4]

So, a price slightly above the ZOPA appears to be a good opening strategy.

BRIDGING THE ZOPA GAP

In addition to helping him develop his opening strategy, Tom feels that this visualization of the ZOPA for his opening offer will give him more confidence to respond to Sue's inevitable negative reactions and eventual counteroffers.

Sue's first reaction will be to protest Tom's high price—other vendors are offering a lower price, she will say. Then she'll ask some questions or comment on the situation. Eventually, however, she will have to make a counteroffer—explicitly with a quantity and price, or implicitly by giving a general indication of her expectations.

Tom knows that Sue's first counteroffer will also have a crucial significance. One possibility is that her first counteroffer to his opening offer of $210 each for 10,000 units is $150, her supposed target price. If this is the case, what final outcome can be expected at the end of the negotiation, after several exchanges?

A common expectation is that the most likely outcome is right in the middle, at $180. This is based on the expression frequently used to conclude an agreement: "Let's split the difference." But Tom was told in WAWS that this expectation is a big mistake in the early stages of a negotiation and should be reserved only for the final move to conclude a long negotiating process that has reached the point of a small, insignificant gap between the two parties.

Apart from this particular endgame case, the "let's split the difference" expression is a strategic mistake for the seller who decides to use it. It does indeed communicate to the buyer that the midpoint is acceptable to the seller, which will often lead to an outright refusal or a counteroffer that is below that midpoint.

If Tom's first offer is at $210, and Sue's first counteroffer at $150, the likely final outcome is indeed somewhere between these two numbers, but more restrictively in the range $172–200 which defines the ZOPA, assuming that Tom's estimate was correct. But the actual agreed price between these two numbers will especially depend on the negotiating skills of each party.

A POOR NEGOTIATION OR AN IMPOSSIBLE DEAL?

Tom is well aware that failure to reach an agreement is the worst possible outcome for a sales negotiation. While both parties want to obtain a favourable conclusion of their negotiation, the outcome that must be avoided by both parties is the complete absence of an agreement.

Considering pragmatically the possibility of such an outcome should help you focus on your negotiating strategy. There are indeed two key reasons why an agreement may not be obtained.

The first reason is a poor negotiation by one or both parties. In Tom's assumptions, both his first offer and Sue's first counteroffer are outside of the ZOPA. If both stick to these first moves and refuse to budge, then they will not be able to reach an agreement. Note also that Sue's expected counteroffer is further outside the ZOPA than Tom's, and the non-advisable split-the-difference approach would result in a price barely above Tom's BATNA. We can safely assume Tom would prefer to obtain a higher price. He would, however, accept the split-the-difference price as a last resort.

While an agreement is preferable for both parties, there is a risk that it may not be reached—even when it was possible—because of a poor negotiation process. The sources of such a failed negotiation can be organized into three categories:[5]

- **Insufficient preparation.** The main elements of primary preparation were covered in Tom's previous WAWS session and the elements of strategy are covered in this one. These should give Tom the key elements and necessary confidence to start a negotiation with good chances of success.

- **Psychological issues.** A sales negotiation takes place in good spirits with the objective of reaching an agreement satisfactory to both parties. It is, however, a battle of minds, with strong personalities involved and potential tense moments. Tom knows that he must feel relaxed, focus on his objective, be attentive to the other person without taking things personally, be assertive but not aggressive, and maintain a healthy dialogue. Failures in the process happen when one or both of the parties are inflexible, hostile, too greedy, or allow their egos to dominate.

- **Inadequate tactics.** Even with the proper preparation and mindset, the tactical interactions during the negotiations remain crucial. Tom knows these issues were covered in WAWS, and he will review this session after he has a good grasp on his strategy.

The other reason for a failed agreement is when a deal is simply impossible. This happens when there is no ZOPA. Tom realizes that this would be the case if Sue's BATNA was $165 instead of $200. In this case, there would be no overlap between his negotiation scope and Sue's. However skilled negotiators Tom and Sue might be, there is no way they could reach an agreement, at least not for a volume of 10,000 units. So, Tom plans to explore other possibilities for different volume levels.

ANTICIPATING THE BUYER'S BATNA FRONTIER

Tom knows that aiming to become a primary supplier for Sue with an order for 10,000 units is an ambitious objective. In his strategy preparation so far, Tom estimated that there is a ZOPA at that volume level and hence the possibility of an agreement if both he and Sue have the negotiation skills and flexibility to make it happen.

There is, however, the possibility that Sue's BATNA is lower than Tom thought and that there is no ZOPA at a volume of 10,000 units. Tom will not find that out until he enters the negotiations and works through a few rounds of offers and counteroffers. But he knows he should prepare himself for this possible outcome.

In addition, even if Sue was ready to accept Tom's firm as a primary supplier with 10,000 units, Tom will have to consider the corporate value that this will generate at the price she would be willing to accept. Maybe Tom would still be able to generate a higher corporate value as a primary supplier at a lower volume, or even as a secondary or tertiary supplier at even lower volumes. It all depends on the prices that Sue would be ready to accept in these different scenarios.

Tom must therefore consider what price levels Sue would be ready to accept for lower volume levels. His experience with other customers tells him that Sue is likely to expect a lower price from the leading supplier, but is ready to accept higher prices for the lower volumes that she would order from a secondary or tertiary supplier in the same category. If there is no room for an agreement at 10,000 units—that is, no ZOPA—his backup strategy is to accept an offer to be a secondary or tertiary supplier with an order at a lower volume level.

To prepare for this possibility and the exchanges that would occur in that direction, Tom knows that he must estimate what Sue's BATNA would be for a greater range of volume levels, even if he must adapt on the fly during his negotiations with her. It's not easy, however, for Tom to put numbers on what is simply a feeling for

Sue's negotiation stance. Regardless, he knows that quantifying a range of possibilities will help him immensely, and so he resolves to make some estimates for a starting scenario.

Tom feels it's unlikely that Sue would buy more than 16,000 units from a single supplier in the coming year. Reviewing similar situations, he estimates that she will first make sure to buy from all suppliers at a price below $260/unit for volumes up to 7,000 units. Beyond this volume level, Tom believes that she will be more aggressive with a primary supplier, expecting a discount of at least $20/unit for each additional increment of 1,000 units. Tom also thought it would be totally unreasonable for Sue to expect a price lower than $120/unit at any volume.

From these estimates, Tom drew a diagram representing his idea of what Sue's BATNA frontier[6] might be (Figure 8.5).

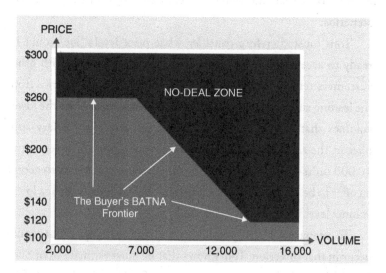

Figure 8.5   The buyer's BATNA frontier.

Exploring the ZOPA Space

Tom next overlaid his own BATNA frontier, which indicated the lower limits for the offers he could make, with Sue's anticipated BATNA frontier, which represented the upper limit of the offer she could accept. He was happy to see that there was a ZOPA[7] between Sue's "No-Deal" zone and his "No-Value" zone. The price range was significant—between $140 and $260—and the volume range wide, from 4,500 to 13,000 units, but the ZOPA was relatively narrow for any given volume level. The scope of the ZOPA was just $40 for a volume of 7,000 units, and half that for a volume of 12,000 units (Figure 8.6).

Tom knew that his strategy should be to find an agreement close to Sue's BATNA frontier. But he also realized that the corporate

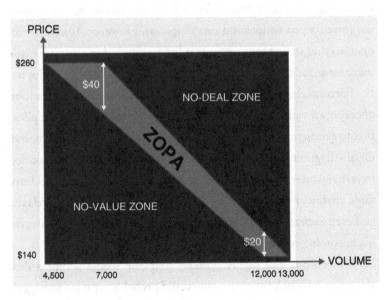

Figure 8.6   The space for agreement.

value he could generate would be different at different points on this frontier. He thus first considered how the three drivers of corporate value evolved along Sue's BATNA frontier.

Obviously, the market share obtained from an agreement would increase with volume, which is why Tom was aiming to become Sue's primary supplier. For profitability, the margin obtained from the agreement would decrease with lower prices, but the total profitability could increase with the additional volume. Customer satisfaction would probably increase as prices decreased, but that would also depend on how the encounter with Sue went.

Tom found that considering the three drivers of corporate value while preparing his negotiation strategy definitely took more reflection than just selling for revenues. He appreciated that the old approach might have led to some excesses in the past, as Tom and his colleagues sought to maximize their commissions, but at least the formula was simple and unambiguous. However, Tom also recognized that selling for corporate value as opposed to revenues made more sense for the firm and all its stakeholders, including employees.

Fortunately, Tom wasn't in the dark when it came to the creation of corporate value. He would be able to use his sales-support application to estimate how corporate value would evolve at different points on his diagram of Sue's anticipated BATNA frontier. Tom decided to just consider the profitability and market-share drivers and leave aside customer satisfaction for the time being. He felt more relaxed and even excited by the idea of using this tool to help him strategize his upcoming session with Sue.

However, it was highly unlikely that Sue would accept a deal along her BATNA frontier—she would probably try hard to negotiate an even better deal for her firm. Tom knew he had to be prepared for a tough negotiation and that his own BATNA frontier set the lower limit on prices he could accept for different volumes. The corporate value he could generate would also vary along this frontier and he should anticipate which direction he would rather move toward if pushed to his limits.

Tom used his sales-support application to see how corporate value evolved as a percentage of his objective along the two frontiers on each side of the ZOPA (Figure 8.7).

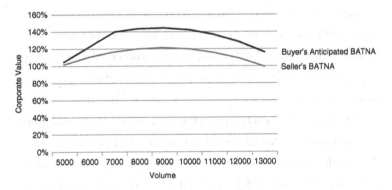

Figure 8.7 Corporate value and the estimated ZOPA.

Looking first at his estimate of Sue's BATNA, Tom was pleased to see that the maximum corporate value at 144 percent of the objective would be achieved at the volume of 9,000 units. This level would combine high profitability with high market share and make ELTRON the primary supplier of MARINTEK for SPCCs.

Tom noticed that corporate value did not decrease significantly between 7,000 and 11,000 units, but on each side on this range, the drop was steeper. However, the corporate value remained above the set objective even in between 5,000 and 13,000 units. All this was quite reassuring to Tom.

If the negotiation was especially tough and converged toward Tom's BATNA frontier, the corporate value generated would obviously be lower. Tom noticed that the maximum achievable value of 120 percent of the objective was at a similar volume level—around 8,000 units. At this level, his firm would still qualify to be Sue's primary supplier. At volumes higher than 11,000 units, the drop in corporate value on his BATNA was steeper for small price differences, and at 13,000 units, it would be below the set objective.

The difference in corporate value between the two BATNA frontiers was somewhat stable at around 20 percent between 7,000 and 12,000 units. But the price gap was $40 for $7,000 units and it narrowed to $20 for 12,000 units. Tom thus observed that the negotiation around higher volumes would be more sensitive and riskier than the negotiation around lower volumes. Tom thus felt more comfortable with a negotiation in the range of 8,000–11,000 units.

After reflecting on all this, Tom considered negotiating an agreement with Sue for a volume of 10,000 units at a price close to her anticipated BATNA of $200 per unit. His sales-support application told him that this would generate a corporate value at 142 percent of the mission given to him, assuming that Sue was also satisfied with the result.

However, Tom suspected that Sue would not settle for a price just at her BATNA, and further that her true BATNA was probably something different than what he had anticipated. He decided he would be happy to settle for 10,000 units at a price of $190 each, which would provide 134 percent of his corporate value objective. Even if he was pushed to his BATNA price of $172 at that volume, the corporate value generated was still at around 120 percent of his objective—a good outcome (see Table 8.1).

Table 8.1 Tom's target considering Sue's expected BATNA for 10,000 units ($).

Deal at	Tom's BATNA	Sue's BATNA	Tom's target
List price	300	300	300
Quantity discount	120	100	110
Price on quantity discount	180	200	190
Discretionary discount	8	0	0
Price offered	172	200	190
Profitability (K$)	720	1,000	900
Corporate value as % of objective	120	142	134

Tom thus defined his negotiation target at $190/unit for 10,000 units. He then decided to make an initial offer of $200 for 11,000 units, allowing him to make concessions to Sue—both on his price and volume ambitions.

SHADOW COACHING

To help Tom and his fellow sales colleagues implement their learnings from the WAWS programme in the sales negotiations that followed, their firm arranged for "shadow coaching." Claudia was assigned to be Tom's coach—she would observe him in action and answer any queries he might have.

What if we could discover how Sue had herself prepared for her encounter with Tom on the other side of the fence? What if we could know what her negotiation guidelines were? In practice, this is a dream scenario that is impossible to reach—we can only make assumptions. But this dream can be made true, exceptionally.

As part of the WAWS follow-up, Claudia interviewed Sue on her preparation for the sales meeting with Tom. Sue shared with her the way she saw the negotiation—confidentially, with the condition that Claudia not reveal her perspective to Tom until after the negotiation was over. Claudia also planned to observe the negotiation when it occurred, without interfering. Afterward, she would debrief both Tom and Sue independently regarding their negotiation experience. Sue agreed to this scenario under the guarantee of confidentiality, knowing that she would also benefit from Claudia's debriefing.

A couple days before his encounter with Sue, Tom shared his negotiation strategy with Claudia. She first checked to make sure that Tom was following the principles presented in the WAWS programme. Claudia was happy to see that Tom defined his BATNA clearly and had a good appreciation of Sue's dispositions. There were, however, some differences between Sue's BATNA frontier as explained by her and as anticipated by Tom, which was unavoidable. Claudia did not reveal any of these differences but asked Tom a number of questions to make sure that he was ready to further investigate Sue's position early in the encounter and adapt his negotiation tactics accordingly.

Claudia was eager to witness the encounter between Tom and Sue. She was particularly keen to see how Tom would use the learning from the WAWS programme to deploy his negotiating tactics—first, to reach an agreement, and even more to reach one that would generate a high corporate value for his firm and a substantial bonus for himself.

After his meeting with Claudia, Tom felt confident that he had done as much preparation as he could on his strategy and that he would be able to adapt it as necessary during his encounter with Sue. He was excited to dive into this negotiation—an important one both for his company, and for himself as a sales pro.

CHAPTER 9

VALUE-CAPTURE TACTICS

The Franciscan monk knocked on the heavy wooden door. When it opened, his armed accomplices rushed in and took over the fortress. The date was January 8, 1297, the man disguised as a monk was Francis Grimaldi, and the place was Monaco.

Now, for more than 700 years, the Grimaldi dynasty has ruled over Monaco. Over this long period, the Grimaldis lost and regained control of the place several times before consolidating their position and building a principality. While one of the smallest nations in the world, Monaco has achieved world prominence in recent times through the Monte Carlo Casino, the wedding of Prince Rainier III with Hollywood actress Grace Kelly in 1956, its Formula 1 Grand Prix, its status as a tourist mecca, and more.

You have likely realized by now that Francis Grimaldi's coup is a great example of value capture, short, medium, and long term! But the point I want to make goes beyond that. Francis Grimaldi obviously had no idea of the long-term consequences of his taking over this fortress on a rock and the creation of this very long dynasty. We do not even know if Grimaldi had a strategy, beyond securing a place that should offer a strong base for protection and expansion.

The increase in visibility and wealth of Monaco under successive rulers is the result of hundreds of specific actions. In addition to the ones mentioned above, we can add the creation of the Oceanographic Museum; the suppression of income, capital, and property tax; and the principality's recent 15-acre expansion over the Mediterranean sea—Mareterra.

The point is that while strategy helps in the preparation for successful action, it is tactics that capture value. Strategy is extremely valuable, but it is purely mental. It does not bring any benefits by itself. Thinkers can have great strategies that bring no value if they are not implemented through tactics. It is tactics that lead to the actions that capture value.

Thinkers love strategy, doers love tactics. Both are crucial! The term *strategy* enjoys prestige and importance, while the word *tactics* often evokes tricks and cunning. The truth is that tactics are undervalued in the common psyche, while they conquer the world.

Moreover, in the thick of the action, the actual tactics that are employed may end up being very different than what was originally anticipated when preparing the strategy. The evolution of events may naturally require minor or major adaptations—and they often do.

While thinking about his coming meeting with Sue, Tom recalled the story of Francis Grimaldi and Monaco, along with the words of his WAWS instructor. Tom went back to the notes he took during the session on tactics for further insights.

THE NEGOTIATION SETTING

We all know the importance of setting in our social interactions with others, and the crucial role it plays in shaping the dynamics and outcomes of those interactions. The negotiation setting can affect the behaviour and attitudes of the individuals involved, as well as their perception of the situation and one another. The negotiation setting can also influence the level of formality and structure in the interaction, as well as the power dynamics and the availability of resources. All these factors can have a significant impact on the relationships between individuals, and ultimately, the success or failure of the negotiation.

So, as a sales pro, you need to have a good understanding of the effect negotiation setting can have on your outcome, and to ensure that it is in your favour and does not work against you. Here are some of the most important aspects of negotiation setting to consider.

INTERACTION MODALITY

This refers to the physical means by which you communicate with your counterpart. The oldest—and to this day, the most effective and preferred—interaction approach is in-person, face to face. Why? Because face-to-face negotiations allow for more persuasive and nuanced communication, including nonverbal cues and gestures, and they can foster a deeper sense of trust and rapport between the parties, which is essential for a successful outcome.

Regardless, for decades, sales pros have relied on telephones to communicate with their counterparts. Phones are quick, ubiquitous, and offer major cost and time savings over traveling to a buyer's location—especially when that location is hours away by car, train, or aeroplane. However, there are also disadvantages to this modality. For example, when you're negotiating by telephone, you miss out on all the nonverbal communication that's going on between you and the other party.

And more recently, video conferencing platforms such as Zoom, Google Meet, and Microsoft Teams have gained in prominence.

These platforms have the advantages of telephone communication plus, since you can actually see the other party—and they can see you—you get some of the advantages of a face-to-face interaction. However, since most people restrict the video stream to just their faces, they miss out on the body language being "spoken" by other parts of their bodies (hands, arms, legs, and so on).

Of course, you could choose to negotiate via email, fax machine (remember those?), letters, text messages, or other asynchronous means, but then you miss out on most every advantage the interaction modalities mentioned above provide.

LOCATION

The location you choose to have your negotiation can also have an effect on the outcome, but only when you are in a face-to-face negotiation. The location of a negotiation can affect the outcome by influencing the perceived power dynamics and emotions of the participants, and creating a certain level of psychological pressure.

In most cases, sales pros will agree to meet the buyer at their site—usually in the buyer's own office or conference room. This confers an advantage to the buyer, who is most comfortable on their own turf and who has all the tools and support they need right there.

Sometimes, however, a sales negotiation may be conducted in the seller's familiar location (e.g., their office, conference room, or even a favourite restaurant) and this is preferable for the sales pro. Again, this confers an advantage to the seller, who gains by being on their own turf—with the tools and support that go along with that—but experienced buyers will usually refuse this proposal.

Ultimately, the parties may agree to meet at a neutral location that negates any advantage that the buyer or seller may have.

NUMBER AND TYPE OF PEOPLE INVOLVED

In the first phase of the selling process, several individuals may be involved on the selling or buying side. This was, for instance, the case when Tom presented ELTRON's E150 to Alan and Pat at MARINTEK. In complex sales situations, teams of several members may be involved on each side when different types of expertise are required to present, evaluate, and specify the offer to be considered.

In the second phase, when the focus is on negotiating the terms of a possible agreement, and other key issues have been addressed and resolved, it is recommended to have just one person on each side of the table. This is what will take place at MARINTEK, where Tom and Sue will each negotiate on their own. Exceptionally, Claudia will be present but just as a passive observer.

TIME AVAILABLE

The time available for a negotiation can have both positive and negative effects. For example, when there's not much time to reach a conclusion, this can increase the sense of urgency and motivation for both parties to reach resolution. This may, in turn, increase the pressure on both sides of the table to make concessions or accept less-favourable terms. When the pressure is particularly high, the buyer or seller may make impulsive decisions, overlook important details, or give in to demands just to reach an agreement.

Similarly, when there is more than ample time to reach a conclusion, this takes the pressure off both parties, giving them the ability to be deliberate and thoughtful in their negotiations. This increases the likelihood that a quality agreement will be reached that both parties will be happy with for the long term.

It's therefore important for sales pros and buyers alike to balance the time to reach a deal with a careful consideration of their goals and priorities. Be sure to have a clear idea of the time available for the negotiation before you start it. It is particularly crucial to aim for closure and not be put under pressure by the unanticipated announcement of the imminent termination of the meeting.

THE ENVIRONMENT

The atmosphere and overall environment of the place where a negotiation is conducted can also have an impact on the behaviour of the participants and the negotiation's ultimate outcome. For example, a professional setting can create a sense of formality, which may cause the participants to also behave more formally with one another, while a relaxed setting can lead to more casual and open discussions. In addition, seating arrangements, temperature, and even lighting can also affect the mood and behaviour of negotiation participants.

Having anticipated the setting for the negotiation, the next step is to anticipate the negotiation's dynamics.

THE NEGOTIATION PATHWAY

When the negotiation gets started, the temptation for action-oriented negotiators is to move on the implementation of their strategy, hopefully crushing any and all opposition they may encounter along the way. However, the application of brute force is never a good approach when it comes to strategy implementation, and even worse so in the context of a negotiation. The British philosopher Sir Francis Bacon expressed it well five centuries ago in his essay, "Of Negotiating": "In all negotiations of difficulty, a man may not look to sow and reap at once; but must prepare business, and so ripen it by degrees."[1]

Bacon expressed with talent what was already known by skilled negotiators long before him. It is indeed a universal and eternal truth that good negotiation takes both time and patience. But, unfortunately, this truth is very often missed, especially in this most crucial phase of value capture which is potentially conflictual and may raise aggressive feelings.

Undeniably, the value-capture phase of a sales negotiation is a zero-sum game, despite all the discourse on "we want a win-win solution" on both sides of the table. The value captured by one party is undeniably not gained by the other. If an agreement is reached, it means that it contains at least some value for each party, hence the "win-win." If this was not the case, there would not be an agreement. But it certainly does not mean that the share of the value that each side captures is equal!

One has to be ready for the tension and the anxieties that will underlie a value-capture negotiation. As we have seen in the previous chapters, a thorough preparation on the primary elements and on strategy is essential to master the inner emotions that could hinder a patient and peaceful deployment of tactics.

But visualizing the pathway to a successful negotiation helps in understanding the various phases involved while appreciating the rhythm required in each. There is indeed a time for casual discussion, for polite enquiries, for suggestions, for standstill silence, and for assertive statements. While one must be sensitive to the specific rhythm of a particular negotiation, following the negotiating pathway in Figure 9.1 can help you patiently manage each stage, which I explore in the sections that follow.

- The *prelude* is the early stage where each party attempts to refine its understanding of the other and set up a favourable setting for the negotiation.

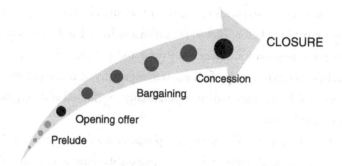

Figure 9.1   The negotiation pathway.

- The *opening offer*, made by either the seller or the buyer, is a crucial point in the negotiation pathway. It is a turning point in the encounter, indicating the end of the gentle discovery time and the start of the crafty contest for value capture.
- This is followed by the *bargaining phase*—a succession of offers, reactions, and counteroffers that explore and probe the existence of a ZOPA and the possibilities that it offers each side.
- Assuming that there is a convergence in the requirements of the two parties, there will still remain a gap that will have to be bridged by a *concession* to reach *closure* and an agreement. The concession and closure stages are addressed in detail in Chapter 10.

THE PRELUDE

The objective of the prelude should be twofold: First, to exchange broad information on each party's requirements to set the stage for a successful negotiation. Second, to assess the personality, attitude, and behaviour of the other party to better interpret his or her reactions during the negotiation.

The tactics to set the stage for a successful negotiation can for the most part be presented as probes and hints.

Probes are questions you'll ask the buyer to investigate their requirements. It's particularly important that you frame these questions in a way that is not perceived as aggressive by the buyer, nor create defensive reactions. They should be open or suggestive at the beginning and become more precise, while being careful to ensure that they are not perceived as entering into the buyer's confidential space.

Price is the most sensitive variable of a sales agreement, and so no specific questions should be raised on price in this initial stage. When you bring up price too early, you risk sparking a defensive reaction or an early challenging demand that may jeopardize the rest of the negotiation.

In addition to making general statements, some specific enquiries you could ask might include: "What do you see as the potential growth in this product category this year?", "What total required volume do you anticipate?", "How many suppliers are you considering?", "Can you share what your expectations are in terms of allowance?"

Such probes are crucial to help you prepare for a negotiation, but they should be submitted at a slow, non-threatening pace. They should not be perceived as a detective investigation or interrogation, but rather as part of a balanced conversation. The best way to achieve this is by volunteering hints.

Hints are pieces of information that you offer to show your desire to reach an agreement, to demonstrate your openness, and to influence the buyer's expectations. Obviously, you do not want to reveal your full information, and especially not any indication of your BATNA, as this would make you very vulnerable in the negotiation. But possible hints could include such things as: "We see that your sector is growing and that your company is gaining share," "We are projecting double-digit growth in our category," "I would like to make all possible efforts to be your primary supplier,""Our approach to allowances is highly competitive." While not revealing any specific numbers, you can even give some hints as to the quantity discount structure practised by your firm.

The other objective of the prelude is for you to assess the personality of the buyer and how you should interpret their negotiating stances. As you will yourself take a position to try to achieve an agreement favourable to your firm and not provide full information, you can expect the buyer to do the same.

Responses by the buyer to probes or hints, as well as to their unsolicited statements in the prelude, are good ways to evaluate their openness, slyness, and flexibility. These are indeed three crucial traits when it comes to sales negotiations.

Openness is the willingness to share information. It shows a higher level of transparency and an inclination to collaborate and is often associated with frankness and honesty. In a negotiation, openness from one party will usually encourage openness from the other party.

Slyness in a negotiation consists in providing a distorted representation of reality to one's advantage. It is strongly advised not to lie in a negotiation, on either side, as this could hurt the negotiator's credibility which is a crucial personal asset. But not providing the total truth already leads to a distortion of reality. Exaggerating one aspect is a common, malicious act in a negotiation. It is short of a pure lie but leads to a specific distortion of reality.

Flexibility in a negotiation indicates the willingness to compromise. It is often mistakenly linked to openness but is an entirely different trait. One can indeed appear to be very open in sharing information but lack flexibility—being very rigid in not moving away from a declared stance.

There is no clear rule to indicate the end of the prelude. On one side, you would like to feel that you have enough information to make an opening offer. On the other side, you do not want the prelude to drag on—you need to reserve sufficient time for the bargaining phase. You will need to judge for yourself when it's time to make an opening offer.

THE OPENING OFFER

In your strategy preparation, you determined your target agreement and the opening offer you should make to reach this target. Considering the new information you were able to gather in the prelude, you may want to revise your opening offer and even to update your target agreement.

After the BATNA and ZOPA, the opening offer is the most important aspect of a negotiation as it creates what is called an anchoring effect. *Anchoring effect* simply means that our judgment is biased based on the starting point of the negotiation. So, your opening offer acts as a mental anchor for the buyer, and it will have a significant effect on the final deal they agree to—more than the subsequent offers and counteroffers. This anchoring effect has repeatedly been documented in a variety of contexts.[2]

It is a commonly held belief that the first party to make an offer is at a disadvantage, that "The first person who speaks loses." This stems from the fact that many negotiations involve multiple ill-defined issues and the value of each of these issues is not clear. In this case, there is the risk for the party making the first offer to grossly under- or over-shoot.

In a sales negotiation, however, each party knows the issues to be discussed and the seller is best placed to know the real value of the offer. So, in the case of sales negotiations, there is no ambiguity: the seller will have an advantage in making the first offer.

An aggressive buyer may jump in and make a low opening offer. This is, however, a risky approach as, in the absence of real information about the seller's commercial guidelines, this "low" opening offer could actually be higher than the intended seller's offer. Or a *really* low first offer by the buyer could create an aggressive response by the seller—leading to a conflictual negotiation, and, eventually, no agreement. If this happens, you indeed have to respond with an equally aggressive counteroffer in the opposite direction.

Ideally, you want your opening offer to be above the buyer's BATNA. Of course, you can't know what this is for certain, but by listening carefully to the answers the buyer gave during the prelude, you will hopefully have some idea of the buyer's BATNA. While you want to make your opening offer high enough, you must be careful not to pitch it too high, otherwise you can trigger negative emotions in the buyer's mind, or even make them feel insulted, which will not be good for the progress of your negotiation.

The key is to make your first offer high but reasonable—ideally, somewhat above the upper end of what you believe the ZOPA to be. Even if they protest, most buyers will respond well to this, because they understand this is part of a good negotiation process. As a seller, starting high (but not too high!) gives you more options for your following moves.

To illustrate the uncertainties in the opening offer, let's take the example of Diana, a sales pro negotiating a quarterly contract for a supply of soft drinks with Steve, the professional buyer at a retail store. As part of their exchanges in the prelude, Steve has already indicated to Diana that he would be interested in ordering 2,000 boxes from her company for Q3, the third quarter. Diana's list price is $21.00/box for up to 1,000 boxes, and her lowest possible price, or BATNA, at 2,000 boxes is $17.00/box. Diana knows how important her opening offer will be in determining the final agreement.

In the previous quarter, Q2, Steve ordered 1,500 boxes at a price of $18.50/box—a slim $0.80 above Diana's then-BATNA of $17.70. After the deal was concluded, Steve indicated that he was very satisfied. Diana was also happy with the agreement but realized, after the fact, that she could have captured more corporate value.

For Q2, the list price was $20.00/box, and in the prelude, Diana told Steve about the various inflationary pressures that forced her company to increase its list price by 5 percent for the current quarter, Q3, to $21.00/box.

Diana realizes that Steve's point of reference is Q2's price of $18.50/box. Since then, two novel elements have occurred: an increase of 5 percent in the list price and an increase in Steve's requirement from 1,500 to 2,000 boxes. This increased volume is lowering Diana's BATNA by $0.70. Bearing that information in mind, what should Diana announce as her opening offer?

Diana knows that there is no exact figure that is the "right" answer to that question. She knows that determining her opening offer is difficult, and that it is a crucial stage in the negotiation. She consequently decides not to focus on the opening offer, but to instead focus on the target price she would like to achieve. Steve paid $18.50/box in Q2 and also knows that the list price has increased by 5 percent for Q3. Using that logic, if Diana simply adds 5 percent to last quarter's price, the current price would be $19.42/unit.

Steve has all this information, so it is fair to assume that he will also be thinking about a figure like $19.42/unit as his maximum price—a higher price would represent a concession on his part. And since he is increasing the order size from 1,500 to 2,000 boxes, it is likely that Steve will ask for an even lower price.

Diana converges at $18.50/unit, the price paid by Steve last quarter, as her *target price*. Her BATNA for Q3 is lower, so that means she is now $1.50 above her BATNA for the same price, rather than the $0.80 she was in the previous quarter. This would certainly be a good result, and it will have a positive impact on corporate value. So, if $18.50/unit becomes her new target price, where should she start the negotiation?

All this considered, Diana decides to use $19.42/unit as her opening offer (see Table 9.1). She has already established that Steve will likely have this figure in mind, and it is easy to see how Diana will explain how she reached that figure as well, by simply adding the 5 percent price increase to the previous quarter's agreement.

Diana anticipates, of course, that Steve will protest (most likely nicely, because he knows this is a fair opening bid). However, Diana has used logic and sound judgment to come up with a fair opening offer, from which she can negotiate toward her target price. Any agreement between the opening and this target price would increase the corporate value captured by Diana compared to Q2 *and* satisfy Steve, as he would have been successful in bargaining a lower price raise than the increase in the list price.

Table 9.1   Diana's logic for her opening offer ($).

	Q2	Q3
Agreement for Q2 order of 1,500 boxes		
List price for 1,000 boxes	20	
Diana's BATNA	17.70	
Price	18.50	
Price minus BATNA	0.80	
Negotiation for Q3 order of 2,000 boxes		
List price for 1,000 boxes		21
Diana's BATNA		17
Diana's target price (Q2 price)		18.50
Target price minus BATNA		1.50
Diana's opening offer (Q2 price + 5%)		19.42
Opening offer minus BATNA		2.41

Setting your opening offer is a matter of judgment based on the information available and your intuition and feeling for the situation. While perfection is not possible, poor openings should be avoided because they can have a negative impact on the rest of the negotiation process. It's the anchoring effect in action.

Some of the consequences of making a poor opening offer could be a loss of trust, a loss of interest from the buyer, a loss of potential corporate value, reputational damage, anger, and even losing the deal completely. Fortunately, these risks and others like them can be greatly reduced thorough preparation.

First, the knowledge of your BATNA based on clear commercial guidelines eliminates the risk of value destruction that could occur when pursuing revenue growth with incentives based on commission. Second, an appreciation of the buyer's BATNA—even if it's not precise—helps to eradicate gross mistakes. And finally, giving repeated attention to the opening offer in your practice will be key in making you an expert sales negotiator.

The Bargaining

After you have pitched your opening offer, you enter the actual bargaining stage of the negotiation. This is like a dance, where you and the buyer go back and forth with reactions, offers, and counteroffers.

Professional buyers are usually well trained not to react positively to an opening offer, nor to readily make a counteroffer. And so, their typical initial response is to refuse the opening offer without making a counteroffer. They might say, "This is totally unacceptable," or "You can do better," or "I expected a lower offer." They intentionally do not provide any sort of information in their statements—their goal is to put sellers in a defensive position and under pressure to improve their offer without any guidance. This is part of the value-capture game, and consequently justifies the seller's gambit of going for opening offers on the high side.

If you the sales pro react by making another offer—trying to fill the void left by the buyer—that would certainly be a mistake. It's a sign of weakness that will later be used and abused against you.

A proper reaction will instead demonstrate that you are fully aware of negotiating tactics and ready to discuss the transaction peacefully—professional to professional, equal to equal. A very relaxed stance, a smile, and a conciliatory remark are more appropriate at this point than a new offer. Acceptable statements include, "I see you are a tough negotiator," "I hope we will be able to reach an agreement despite your reaction," or "There are different ways we can search for an agreement, but I need more guidance on your part."

This is where you start to establish your territory and your credibility as a negotiator. Your statements should be assertive but not aggressive. So that you feel at ease, they should reflect your own personality and not be copied from someone else—least of all from a generic negotiation workbook.

After a few rounds of exchanges to establish a balanced bargaining relationship, it would be best for the buyer to make a counteroffer. If this is not the case, however, you may need to make a new offer. This new offer could possibly be on a different basis, such as a different volume level or some other element such as an allowance. Because it comes after you have shown your negotiation skills, this new offer is an invitation to the buyer to take over with a counteroffer.

If the buyer still totally refutes the offer and refuses to make a proposition in return, you will need to increase your assertiveness level and possibly escalate the confrontation. The risk is that the negotiation will be interrupted, but sometimes this is the best resolution when you've reached a dead end because it avoids the possibility of making a very unfavourable deal. If there was genuine interest in your offer, it's likely that the negotiation will resume at a later time and on more level and positive grounds. It's the equivalent of turning down a car salesperson's "best" offer and walking out the door. You soon discover that it wasn't really their best offer when the salesperson chases you down in the parking lot to make a better one.

When a counteroffer is finally made by the buyer, it is likely to be significantly lower than your opening offer. This is when the constructive exploration of the ZOPA takes place, including a possible revision of your estimate of the buyer's BATNA frontier.

When backtracking on an offer, do it by very small steps—especially on price, and even on volume. Do not hesitate, however, to consider making a counteroffer at a significantly different volume level. This may be a very good way to get out of an unproductive negotiating path, to destabilize the buyer, or to explore another part of the ZOPA.

Your succession of moves should aim at stirring in the direction of your intended target agreement or possibly of a newly revised target. You should keep some room for concessions—for instance, in terms of an allowance—that you will use in the final stages of closure.

In Chapter 10, we will look at these final stages of the negotiation in greater depth. Before we get to that discussion, however, let's first review two of the most important aspects that are of great value throughout the entire negotiation pathway to refine your tactics: active listening and body language.

ACTIVE LISTENING

You've probably heard of the technique known as active listening, but what exactly is it and how can it help you in your sales negotiations? *Active listening* is when we do more than just hear the words that someone is saying to us. In their 1957 book, *Active Listening*, psychologists Carl Rogers and Richard Farson explained that they called this kind of listening *active* listening

> ...because the listener has a very definite responsibility. He does not passively absorb the words which are spoken to him. He actively tries to grasp the facts and the feelings in what he hears, and he tries, by his listening, to help the speaker work out his own problems.[3]

In the time since the concept of active listening was presented to the public by Rogers and Farson in their book, it has become one of the most important subjects in communications. During a sales negotiation, the main goals of active listening are to ensure points are well understood and to project a well-assured, cooperative stance.

Here are some key aspects of active listening:

- **Listen intensely.** Without judgment and without interruption. When many of us listen to others, we are only hearing some and not all the words they are saying. This is because, at the same time we are listening to the other person, we are also listening to the stream of self-talk going through our own minds. Clear your mind of the things that may be distracting you and listen *intensely* to the other person.
- **Focus on the speaker.** Show that your attention is focused and undivided on the person in front of you. You can do this by giving encouraging verbal cues to the other person, such as "I see," "Yes, I understand," and "I get it." You can also do this by giving encouraging nonverbal cues, including body language, which we

will explore in the next section. When the speaker knows you are truly focused on them and what they are saying, you build trust and rapport as you strengthen your relationship.

- **Ask questions.** Another important active listening technique is to ask questions that clarify or expand your understanding. Not only does this show the speaker that you really are listening to what they are saying, it also ensures you get as much out of the conversation as you can. For example, "I'm not sure I understand the point you just made, would you please explain it in more detail?" or "Could you please give me a bit more background on why your company has given you those guidelines?" or "Why did you decide to take that approach?" Just be sure that the questions you ask are neither critical nor defensive, which would likely cause the speaker to withdraw inward or respond in kind.

- **Repeat what you heard.** One of the best ways to confirm the accuracy of what the person said to you—while showing them that you are engaged in what they are saying and listening actively—is to repeat what you heard. For example, "I believe you just said that you want to triple your buy from 10,000 to 30,000 units—did I get that right?" or "I think I heard you say that price is your biggest concern," or "Did you say that if we can get to your price and quantity, you would be willing to sign an agreement today?"

Make active listening an essential tool in your sales negotiation toolbox. The benefits are many, including gaining more accurate information, building better and stronger relationships with your counterparts, and ultimately, negotiating deals that capture the highest levels of corporate value.

Body Language

In Chapter 5, we explored how we communicate with one another both verbally and nonverbally. We also discussed the findings of psychologist Albert Mehrabian, who found that verbal communication was significantly less important than nonverbal—the body language, gestures, and other cues we deliver to convey meaning. Several studies indicate that in many face-to-face conversations, the nonverbal dimension is the most important part of the communication.[4] Let's now focus on just one component of nonverbal communication: body language.

Body language includes such things as posture, gestures, facial expressions, and eye contact. In just one example, our faces can express and convey a wide range of emotions and attitudes, such as happiness, sadness, anger, and surprise. While important in any communication, interpreting and expressing your thoughts, attitudes, and emotions through body language—and being able to accurately interpret them when expressed by your counterpart—form a crucial skill in any sales negotiation to detect, reinforce, test, and even destabilize.

In his *Dictionary of Body Language*,[5] author Joe Navarro identifies more than 400 postures and their significance—from head to toe. Here are some examples of commonly used body positions and what they communicate:

- Leaning in: Interest, attentiveness, or engagement
- Leaning back: Detachment, disinterest, or skepticism
- Arms crossed: Discomfort, defensiveness, or resistance
- Arms open: Approval, openness, or acceptance
- Making eye contact: Interest, attention, or honesty
- Avoiding eye contact: Discomfort, shame, or dishonesty
- Fidgeting: Discomfort, nervousness, or boredom

The list goes on and on. Keep in mind that body language varies from culture to culture and that there is also variation between individuals. While in some cultures, making direct eye contact is seen as a sign of honesty, in other cultures, it may be interpreted as rude, angry, or aggressive. And while crossing one's arms can communicate discomfort, defensiveness, or resistance, it can also indicate that someone is simply cold.

If you are attentive to these cultural or situational specificities, in the case of a contradiction between the words a buyer is saying and their body language, which should you trust? Body language, always. As Mehrabian—the expert on the subject—says, "When there are inconsistencies between attitudes communicated verbally and posturally, the postural component should dominate in determining the total attitude that is inferred."[6]

The same is also true in reverse. Make sure that your body language is in line with your verbal communication, with the exception of those times when you choose to remain silent and respond to buyers' communication only through body language.

Body language is particularly important in face-to-face meetings, where you can see your counterpart's entire body—and they can see yours. In virtual sales meetings, many of the body postures are not visible and so you lose out on a significant portion of what is being communicated. On the other hand, facial expressions are more visible than in face-to-face meetings because the camera is often zoomed in on the participants' faces.

But even when you're engaged in discussions by telephone, if you give full attention to the tone of your counterpart's voice, you can often detect valuable signals. With experience, some claim that they can see a smile or a frowning face through the phone!

PUTTING ALL THIS INTO ACTION

Let's return to Tom and his upcoming sales negotiation with Sue. After reviewing his WAWS session on tactics, Tom met with Claudia, his coach, and he described the strategy and tactics he planned to use in his encounter with Sue.

Claudia was very supportive. She asked a few questions, then emphasized that this was Tom's meeting and that she would only passively observe the proceedings. Her objective was to debrief Tom after the meeting was concluded, as a follow-up to the WAWS programme. Claudia's sole suggestion to Tom was that he should ask Sue for a short break before closing the meeting, so that he would have some time to reflect on what had transpired before entering the final stage of the negotiation.

Tom thought this was a great idea. Sue had agreed to a 90-minute meeting, so Tom decided to try for a 10-minute break after about one hour.

On the big day, Tom and Claudia arrived together early at MARINTEK. After registering at the reception desk, they were led through a corridor with eight meeting rooms and maybe a dozen chairs with people waiting. Claudia told Tom that the people in the chairs were probably all sales pros waiting to be called into one of the meeting rooms for a negotiation with a professional buyer.

Indeed, it seemed to be procurement day at MARINTEK. Claudia told Tom that the purpose of this setting—with the chairs arranged in the corridor—was probably to intimidate salespeople before their negotiations commenced. They both laughed, as one of the sessions in the WAWS programme was devoted to breathing techniques that could help control one's anxieties when put under pressure.

A few moments later, a woman popped her head out of one of the meeting rooms and asked if the people from ELTRON had arrived. Having previously met Sue, Claudia knew that Sue had recognized her but that she was keeping to her formal approach.

After they settled into the meeting room, Sue welcomed them warmly. She then initiated an informal discussion, asking them a variety of questions, including if they found the location easily, if they were well treated at reception, how was life at ELTRON, and if they had any boating experience. She also mentioned how much she enjoyed boating herself and that working at MARINTEK was a real treat.

Tom did not dare to ask Sue any questions at this stage to avoid making a misstep that would reflect badly on him. Sue was so casual that Tom could not escape thinking that Alan must have been joking when he referred to her as "the shark."

But, of course, they were just getting started.

After this pleasant introductory discussion, Sue indicated that she had been briefed by Alan and Pat who approved the E150 for purchase, as well as three other SPCCs that had similar characteristics and were produced by other manufacturers. Tom knew, however, that Alan had recognized that the E150 was somewhat superior to its competitors on several dimensions. Sue said that she was not interested in hearing about any of the great benefits of the E150 and stressed that she was only concerned about negotiating the terms of a fair agreement.

Tom indicated that he agreed completely with the purpose of the meeting. He then asked Sue if they still had about 90 minutes for the meeting, and if they could have a break at some point, to which she agreed.

Tom then engaged in an exploratory discussion with Sue, during which time they exchanged various hints without divulging any essential information. Tom indicated that the E150 was very successful in a wide variety of applications and that ELTRON was now penetrating the pleasure boat market. The company's products were leading edge, and their increased scale of production allowed them to achieve a very reasonable cost level. He explained that he would do his best to become MARINTEK's primary supplier for SPCCs.

Sue confirmed that the pleasure boat market was indeed booming and that MARINTEK was gaining share. It was important to the company that they retain an edge in innovation while keeping their prices competitive. She mentioned that she had to secure the supply of 20,000 SPCCs for the next model year. Tom noticed that this was on the high end of Pat's projection.

During this exchange, Tom observed that Sue had progressively moved from her initially pleasant posture to one that was increasingly more assertive. He noticed in particular her steady voice and the way she looked at him—firmly, with no hint of uncertainty. Tom could feel from Sue's demeanour that she was about to make a decisive move, and indeed, she unexpectedly announced that $160 was her target price for an SPCC bought in large volume. This took Tom by surprise as he had planned to plant the anchor with his opening offer.

Tom had set his opening offer at $200 for 11,000 units, but he now felt that he needed more negotiating room, given this first exchange and Sue's posture. He decided that starting with the same price of $200 but for 12,000 units was more appropriate, while keeping in mind his target agreement at $190 for 10,000 units. This is thus the opening offer he made to Sue while looking intensely at her.

As expected, Sue protested that this offer was not acceptable, without giving any justification nor making a counteroffer. Tom noticed, however, a glimpse of satisfaction in her eyes that did not fit with her statement. He did not know if this was just expressing the pleasure she felt when entering into a fight that she enjoyed, or if his opening offer reassured her. In any case, he knew that he should not fall into the trap of improving his offer right away. Instead, he justified that his offer was a fair one, considering the high volume and the desire to be the primary SPCC supplier for MARINTEK.

After being pushed back by Sue several times, and asking her without success to make a counter-proposal, he mentioned in succession the high innovation content of the E150, the inflationary costs affecting the industry, the fact that her price references could be outdated, and a few other points that he had carefully prepared. When Tom felt that Sue was becoming annoyed by his presentation of these points, he shifted gears—suggesting that he could give her some financial allowance to help with the training of the engineers on the E150 or its insertion in the MARINTEK promotional materials for the new model boats.

Sue responded that she was not interested in discussing an allowance at this point, but that she just wanted a better price. Tom noted that Sue did not completely close the door to the idea of an allowance at a later time.

Tom then proposed that he would agree to reduce the volume down to 8,000 units if she thought that he had been too ambitious in his offer. Sue stressed that volume was not the issue for her but instead that it was price. Tom reacted by saying that the price offered was based on a volume of 12,000 units but that he could consider making an exceptional effort to offer the same price for a reduced volume of 10,000 units. Tom noticed a change in Sue's posture and even a very slight smile.

She repeated, however, that price was the key issue, and that for 10,000 units, she would not accept paying more than $170 per unit. Tom was relieved that Sue finally had reached the point where she was willing to make a constructive counteroffer. He made a slightly better offer for the same 10,000 units, to which Sue reacted by indicating that she could consider a higher volume for a better price. After a few more exchanges, the bargaining had moved to a volume of 11,000 units.

In their final exchange, Tom proposed a price of $180 and Sue's last offer was at $175 (see Table 9.2 for a summary of their negotiation). Tom checked his sales-support application which confirmed that at these prices the corporate value generated was above 130 percent of his objective.

Table 9.2   Tom and Sue's negotiation summary.

Sue's moves	Tom's moves
Prelude	
Casual friendly tone	Casual friendly tone
Interested in terms only	E150 very successful
Boat market booming	Entering boat market
Innovation focus	Reasonable cost
Need 20,000 units	Desire to be primary supplier
Opening offer	
$160 for "large volume"	
Bargaining	
	$200 for 12,000 units
Protest	Innovation
Push back	Inflation
Push back	Price references outdated
Push back	Allowance possibility
No allowance at this point	Consider 8,000 units
Price is the issue, not volume	$200 for 10,000 units
$170 for 10,000 units	$198 for 10,000 units
Higher volume for a better price	
[...]	
Position before pausing	
$175 for 11,000 units	$180 for 11,000 units

Tom anticipated, however, that Sue would come back at the last minute with an allowance request that could hurt his corporate value, and hence his bonus. While the hardest part of the negotiation was completed, Tom knew he should be very careful about closing the deal. He suggested to Sue that they take a short break, which she accepted.

TAKING A BREAK

Claudia had quietly observed the meeting, making sure that her posture and other body language remained neutral to avoid influencing Tom or Sue. But she had been busy taking *lots* of notes!

As they walked together to the lobby, Claudia told Tom that he had done well but that she did not want to give him any further feedback until the meeting was completely over. For the time being, she would rather let him quietly reflect on the negotiation so far and prepare for closure of a deal.

CHAPTER 10

VALUE-CAPTURE CLOSURE

Closing a deal is always a special event. Big or small, it should be celebrated as a victory because the line between closing a deal and losing it is sometimes very thin. Indeed, one of the most important closures in business history happened on November 6, 1980, for the relatively small sum of $430,000. I hear you saying, "That's not so big, there have been thousands of bigger deals." And that may well be true on the surface, but I urge you to look a little deeper.

Remember the short-, medium-, and long-term dimensions of corporate value we discussed earlier? The above deal was signed by two young men—Bill Gates and Paul Allen—to develop the operating system that IBM needed for its new personal computer (PC).[1] Microsoft was only a few years old at the time, and still a small business specializing in computer-language compilers. This non-exclusive deal with IBM transformed the future of Microsoft, making it the world's largest software company while catapulting Bill Gates and Paul Allen into the ranks of the world's richest billionaires.

When IBM first approached Microsoft, however, Bill Gates and Paul Allen did not have the solution to the problem. But they had one lead—a Seattle-area company that had developed the 86-DOS operating system—and the confidence that they would deliver it.

They signed the deal, taking a risk and knowing that they had little to lose but much to gain.

Ironically, Microsoft was not IBM's first choice. The company had first approached Digital Research, which was then the leading provider of operating systems for microcomputers. However, when Digital Research refused to sign IBM's non-disclosure agreement, IBM turned to Microsoft for a solution. Digital Research was eventually purchased by Novell for $80 million in 1991. Microsoft's revenue for its 1991 fiscal year? $1.8 billion.

One deal lost, one closed, two different destinies.

ALWAYS BE CLOSING

There is no sale until it is closed. There is no such thing as a 99 percent-closed deal—either it is, or it is not. Every salesperson knows this fundamental axiom of sales, and their commissions reflect its truth.

Even when salespeople were best known for peddling products to unwilling customers, closure was emphasized as key. It was the ABC of selling—"Always be closing"—made famous in the 1992 film, *Glengarry Glen Ross*, by sales trainer Blake in his verbally abusive motivational speech.[2] Salespeople practiced "closing phrases" to push customers into signing and avoid the "I like it but give me time to think about this" or any other delay that could allow the sale a chance to escape.

They also used (and still use today in some businesses) a variety of closing tactics such as claiming scarcity—that only a few items were left in stock—or that the offer was valid for only 24 hours. A house may have been on the market for several months, but when you express an interest in buying it, the real estate agent is likely to tell you that somebody else is ready to make an offer, so you had better hurry.

These pushy closing tactics, often used against credulous consumers, reflected the times of seller power. They may have been effective in gaining sales, but they gave the sales profession a bad reputation.

Obsession with closing can indeed lead to deals that should not have been made. Even if they brought revenues to the selling firm, and commissions to the sales reps, deals made with the pushy tactics described above can have substantial related costs. The first obvious one is human, as they often create problems for the buyers who, to preserve their own interests, should not have made the purchase. Maybe they spent more than they could afford (they bought a car loaded with all the options instead of the basic model), or they bought something they didn't need.

Another related cost is reputational, both for the firm and the sales rep as negative word of mouth is spread by disappointed, unwilling buyers that can hurt their future activities. You can find ample examples of this in online consumer reviews posted to platforms such as Yelp and Google reviews, where disgruntled customers talk about how some overly zealous car (or solar power, or cable television, or you name it) salesperson pushed them into a deal they should not have made. As the 1-star reviews pile up for such tactics, any business is sure to suffer the negative consequences.

The third cost is legal. When there is a lot of money on the line, some buyers placed in damaging situations by these pushy tactics may decide to take their case to court. This can cause significant financial harm to businesses that engage in these tactics as they are forced to unwind the deals and pay legal costs.

In business situations where professional buyers are less credulous, such pushy sales tactics are rare, but some deals should never have been closed for the very reason that is central to the 3rd sales transformation: Because they destroyed corporate value.

When in Chapter 3 we introduced the move toward an increased focus on corporate value, we indicated that this change was in great part a reaction to the previous strategic emphasis by corporations on revenue growth at all costs. Salespeople were incentivized using a revenue-based commission scheme, which induced them to give strong discounts to close a sale—whatever it took. Such deals often resulted in corporate-value destruction, unbeknown to the salespeople who did not have access to financial information and were acting rationally based on their incentive programmes.

So, the real objective should not be ABC—always be closing—but instead, *always be closing good deals.* That means closing deals that create corporate value in the short, medium, and long term. This is achieved with deals that provide a balance of profitability, market share, and customer satisfaction.

CLOSING THE TWO SELLING PHASES

Closure in modern business selling is certainly softer and more sophisticated than in the old days. But it is more important than ever. Why? Because this is when everything converges. It's the point at which you can win or lose. It is the finish line, and there is always the possibility that you could leave a sales encounter with nothing to show for your efforts. And that's a disappointing (and unacceptable) place for any sales pro to find themselves in.

If the offer is a simple product or service sold at *a fixed nonnegotiable price,* the goal of closure is just to transform a buyer's interest into a decision to buy. This is achieved by demonstrating the value of the offer to the customer, and the sales focus is on the *creation of perceived consumer value*. If the customer develops a willingness to pay (WTP) above the announced fixed price, he or she perceives that this offer is "good value for money."

Imagine a business that wants to buy a few computers from their local Apple Store. They were willing to pay up to $4,200 for each desktop computer but were delighted when the sales specialist showed them a computer with a fixed, retail price of $3,500 that did everything the company needed. So, they happily bought several. In this case, there is a sale which determines closure. There is no further negotiation.

For most business products and services, complex or simple, there are two phases of the selling process, each with its own closure. In the first phase of the sales process, the sales pro's first objective is to gain the buyer's interest in the offer. As for the simple straight sale above, this is achieved by demonstrating the value that it represents for the customer who develops a WTP above the basic conditions which remain to be negotiated.

The successful closure of the first selling phase occurs when the offer is approved to enter the second selling phase, where the terms of an agreement are negotiated. This second phase is our focus and is about the *creation of corporate value* or *value capture*. Closure of this phase is an agreement specifying the terms of a sale.

The purpose of all the work completed by the sales professional for a sales negotiation—including preparation and the development of strategy and tactics—is to achieve closure. It is at this crucial point of closure that everything converges. It is the acid test of the application of the value-capture concepts and techniques in a context of uncertainties.

All three phases of value capture—preparation, strategy, and tactics—have a twofold objective: to reduce your uncertainties while increasing the chances of a favourable closure, and to move the negotiation toward a position that is favourable for you.

The phase of negotiation tactics for value capture seen in Chapter 9 is the last chance for you to resolve some of the remaining uncertainties by exploring the ZOPA in your negotiations with the buyer. But you will still have to live with uncertainties as you reach a negotiation's closure.

What kinds of uncertainties can you expect to encounter?

For one, you won't have a complete picture of the buyer's decision-making process—that will remain hidden during the course of your negotiation. In addition, you'll be uncertain about the inherent biases of the information provided by the buyer. Are they being completely transparent with you, or are they holding back information to retain an advantage? Finally, you won't know how ready the buyer is to accept a compromise.

In short, you won't have certainty over the buyer's objective and BATNA frontier, which determine their negotiation space. Even if you have a better understanding of these issues than when you set your strategy, your last moves will have to be made facing the remaining uncertainties and taking some risks. It is about exercising judgment while dealing with these uncertainties. Make no mistake, it's not easy. But this is a tremendously valuable leadership skill to develop—one that will make you a winner.

As you reach the point of closure, there is no guarantee that you have explored all the possibilities in the ZOPA—your ability to test the possible options was constrained by the buyer. Indeed, as it's often said in negotiations, "it takes two to tango." You can assume that the buyer has a genuine interest in exploring options to find an agreement, but they want to do this around *your* BATNA frontier rather than *their* BATNA frontier.[3]

So, where exactly are you as you begin to get the strong feeling that you are approaching closure?

BRIDGING THE GAP

As you perceive that you are approaching closure, you should realize that there remains either a small or a significant gap between the buyer's position and yours. Let's look at these two possible situations in turn.

When you feel that there is only a small gap between your last offer and the buyer's response, it means that you are within the ZOPA, and you know that an agreement is within easy reach. You do not know how far you are from the buyer's BATNA frontier and if there is the possibility of obtaining a better deal. But it is now too late for these considerations—they will only distract your attention at this point.

In addition, if you start focusing on the possibility that you could have reached a better deal, and that you now regret some of your negotiating moves, you run the risk that your ego will get in the way of a successful closing. Any temptation to capture more value at this stage—for instance, by backtracking directly or indirectly to a higher price—would not only be totally rejected by any buyer but would also give you the reputation of an untrustworthy negotiator. If you reached this stage, it's because you know that your last offer is above your BATNA frontier and that it produces an acceptable corporate value.

The only consideration that should have your total attention at this point is how to bridge the gap that remains between you and the buyer to reach closure.

The easy approach is simply to accept the buyer's last counteroffer. If the gap is small, your sales-support application will likely confirm that the value you will capture is quite acceptable and not that different from the one corresponding to your last offer. But savvy sales pros know it is always worth taking the time to sharpen your last moves to closure. With the sale now being practically secured, your attention can move to how to use these last moves to develop a positive reaction from the buyer *and* build a stronger relationship for future sales negotiations.

The customer satisfaction principles presented in Chapter 5—which definitely help in the tactics for value capture—now take on their ultimate importance. It is particularly advisable at this point to make a concession and agree with the last move to be made by the buyer. At the same time, you must consider the impact of this concession on corporate value. The sharpened closure moves consist of making the concession that has the biggest positive impact on the buyer's satisfaction *and* the lowest negative impact on the value captured.

From the business acumen section of Chapter 6, "The Leadership Attitude," we learned that the allowance (covering all secondary negotiation variables) is usually the best variable to use for a move when approaching closure. The buyer will probably negotiate a better set of terms than the allowance offered, and if necessary, after a few exchanges, closure should be obtained by accepting the last acceptable buyer's request on allowance.

However, it's a totally different situation when a significant gap still exists as you approach closure. You may ask yourself, "Why would I feel that I am approaching closure when there is still a significant gap between my last offer and the buyer's counteroffer?" This is a fair question, as the aim of the bargaining phase is to converge toward a focal point of agreement, and one should not usually envision closure when large differences still exist. This may, however, be necessary in at least three situations.

The first is when you are getting close to the end of a time limit that has been previously agreed to for the negotiation. The second is when you sense impatience from the buyer who, implicitly or explicitly, wants to conclude the encounter. The third is when you have reached a point of total deadlock, and the buyer does not want to make any change in their last counteroffer—despite making several adjustments yourself.

At this final stage, it is *not* advisable to change both volume and price, as this would create confusion with the buyer at a time when a clear resolution must be obtained. There is thus no longer a consideration of exploring the BATNA frontiers but rather to concentrate on the buyer's BATNA for the volume being considered. Whatever the reason for which you sense that the bargaining phase has come to an end, you should realize that the significant remaining gap comes from either the absence of a ZOPA, or a stubborn attempt by the buyer to capture a stronger share of the value. You cannot know which of these two reasons is the real one because you do not know the buyer's BATNA. But there are three important elements to consider when deciding on your last moves.

First, you will know if the buyer's last counter-move is below or above your BATNA. When the buyer's last counter-move is below your BATNA, you are in what I call the RED space illustrated in Figure 10.1. I call it the RED space because you will have to be somewhat aggressive to explore if the buyer is ready to accept an offer above your BATNA, and thus if the buyer's BATNA is above yours. To achieve this, you may have to compromise the customer's satisfaction in exchange to determine if there is or is not the possibility of an agreement. This is the most worrying closure situation for the sales pro as it maintains the uncertainty around the existence of a ZOPA, and hence of an agreement.

When, on the other hand, the buyer's last counter-move is above your BATNA, you are in what I call the BLUE space. Here, you are sure that there is a ZOPA and hence the possibility of an agreement despite the large remaining gap. I call it the BLUE space because you can safely explore the remaining price gap without taking an aggressive stance. While showing your muscles, you should monitor the buyer's satisfaction and ensure the possibility of a recovery in case they are unhappy with how the negotiation is proceeding.

Second, you will also know what pricing slack you still have in your last offer above your BATNA for the volume considered. This slack provides you with a range of pricing latitude for your last moves. The decision for your last move is thus which portion of your pricing slack to forgive in an attempt to close a deal. At one extreme, you can give away all your pricing slack and move down to the buyer's offer in the BLUE space or to your BATNA in the RED space. At the other extreme, you can give away little or none of that pricing slack.

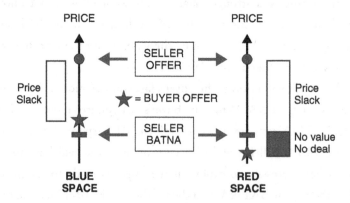

Figure 10.1   Are you in the BLUE or RED space?

Third, you should have by this point developed an informed appreciation of the buyer with whom you have been negotiating, especially on each of the three dimensions highlighted in Chapter 9: openness, slyness, and flexibility. If you feel that your buyer has been open, straight, and flexible, you should be more inclined to believe that their position reflects a real requirement, probably with somewhat of a negotiation margin. If, at the other end, you feel that your buyer has been uncooperative and exaggerating their demands, you can assume that they are likely to still have significant price latitude and that you can play your last moves harder.

When you make your last moves toward closure, still facing a significant gap, these three elements must be considered: Are you in the RED or the BLUE space? What is your pricing slack? What is the negotiating style of your buyer? And then you will have to jump into the unknown with your best, educated judgment—taking risks while expressing the confidence that you have gained through your extensive experience negotiating similar deals during the course of your career.

But before you jump into the unknown to find closure, let's first look at the big picture using the closure map.

THE CLOSURE MAP

The *closure map* is a concept I developed to better visualize the bargaining and closure phases of value capture in sales. We presented it in part when introducing the ZOPA in Chapter 8, "Value-Capture Strategy." The closure map in Figure 10.2 represents a generalized picture for discussing the principles of closure and is not for a specific sales negotiation.

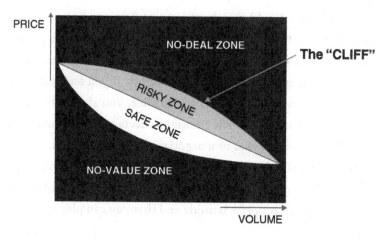

Figure 10.2   The closure map.

The closure map contains the two variables that are usually key in any sales negotiation: volume and price. If volume and price are not the most relevant in a specific situation, they should be replaced by the two most important negotiation variables. Any other less-important variables are not considered at this stage and come more into focus in the last stage to make the concessions required to finalize closure. We have regrouped these less-important variables in what we called *allowance*.

At the bottom of the closure map is the *no-value zone*. This simply means that for a given volume level, the price is simply too low to deliver any corporate value. The line limiting the no-value zone upward is your BATNA frontier. There is no uncertainty about this line as it is determined by your commercial guidelines, taking into account the maximum quantity discount and any other discretionary discount available to you. These guidelines ensure that any offer above this line will create corporate value. But obviously, you will try to negotiate a deal as much as possible above your BATNA frontier as this will generate a higher corporate value.

At the top of the closure map is the *no-deal zone*—any offer in this zone will be refused by the buyer. This is because the line limiting the no-deal zone is the buyer's BATNA frontier. You do not know the exact position of this BATNA frontier, and this is your biggest source of uncertainty. It is determined by the buyer's procurement policy, probably following guidelines set by their company. This BATNA frontier ensures that the buyer will make deals that create value for their company. However, the buyer will try to negotiate a deal as much as possible below their BATNA frontier as this will generate a higher value for their company.

Between the no-value and no-deal zones is the ZOPA. While you only know for sure the bottom end of the ZOPA, because it is your own BATNA frontier, you can visualize that the closer you come to the buyer's BATNA, the higher risk you take.

The lower part of the ZOPA is marked as the *safe zone*. The corporate value you can capture there is positive but lower than it could be. If you move up on the closure map, the corporate value you can generate will increase, but you will eventually enter what is called the *risky zone*. This is where your rewards are highest, but if you go too far, you may fall off *the cliff*. This is where you enter the no-deal zone and will fail to close an agreement.

A closure map is purely conceptual as you do not know the buyer's BATNA frontier, but it provides a structure to better understand the best negotiation tactics for value capture, and especially, to make an educated judgment as you approach closure.

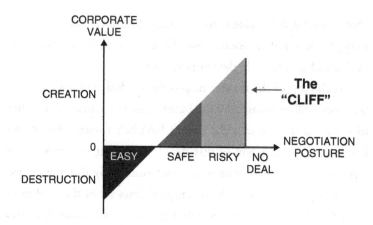

Figure 10.3   The negotiation posture.

As one moves up the closure map, the general relationship between corporate value and the seller's negotiation posture is indicated in Figure 10.3. On the left is the *easy* posture, when you accept a buyer's requirements while destroying corporate value in terms of profitability, market share, or customer satisfaction. This is what sometimes happened when the key objective was gaining revenues and sales were incentivized on commission.

With a focus on corporate-value creation and related commercial guidelines, this situation is now clearly prevented. As you move above the seller's BATNA, the corporate value generated increases, first, in the safe zone and then in the risky zone. Figure 10.3 clearly illustrates the classical business investment choice: lower risk and lower returns versus higher risk and higher returns. The magical dream of low risk and high returns seldom exists, but you can reduce your risks by using a structured approach to help guide your judgment.

Managing Risk at Closure

When making decisions as you face uncertainties, it is impossible to be perfectly right all the time. Winning in this context is when you have a high success rate, that is, when your outcome is above a set objective or higher than your competitors. This requires a combination of two skills: a structured approach and managing risk. This is true of business leaders, investors, medical doctors, golfers, card players, and many other experts operating in an uncertain environment.

In terms of value-capture selling, we have already gone through the techniques that will provide you with a structured approach. Concerning risk management, some people love the mental exercise of estimating uncertain outcomes when playing card games or betting. Others are scared or even hate having to face these uncertain outcomes. Regardless, in value-capture selling, one needs to be familiar with a few basic risk-management principles.

The first principle is probabilistic. If you are facing an outcome for which you estimate a probability, you should consider that the expected outcome is its value multiplied by the probability that it occurs. For instance, if you think that there is a 60 percent probability that you will receive a bonus of $5,000, or nothing, your expected bonus is calculated to be $3,000. There are other principles of risk management that you should also consider applying, including the highest risk, the lowest risk, and the possibility of recovery or adjustment after the event at risk.

All these risk-management principles are important as you approach closure. Let's look at how they work by way of a couple of case stories.

Ann has spent the last 90 minutes in a sales negotiation meeting with Scott, a professional buyer, and she senses that she is nearing closure. For the unit volume she is considering, her last offer to Scott was $16 per unit with an allowance of $10,000. Scott has made a counteroffer at $15, improving on his last position of $14.50. Ann's sales-support application tells her that this number would generate a corporate-value outcome that results in a $3,000 bonus.

If she accepted Scott's offer, Ann would be in the safe zone, but she thinks she can do better and is therefore considering making one last offer. This final offer would maintain her previous price of $16 but increase the allowance to $15,000. This would generate a significantly higher corporate value, resulting in a $6,000 bonus—double the number she would get by simply accepting Scott's latest offer (see Ann's probabilistic choices in Table 10.1).

If she makes this offer, Ann knows she will move into the risky zone. However, she has carefully observed Scott during their bargaining exchanges, and she believes that there is an 80 percent chance he would accept it. Ann must choose between making this final offer or accepting Scott's counteroffer. Which of the two options do you think she should choose?

The offer Ann is thinking about making would give her a $6,000 bonus with a probability of 80 percent, which works out to an expected value of $4,800. This is superior to the $3,000 she is

Table 10.1 Ann's probabilistic choices ($).

	Price	Allowance	Ann's bonus	Probability of closure (%)
Ann, the seller	16	10,000		
Scott, the buyer	15	10,000	3,000	100
Ann, the seller	16	15,000	6,000	80

certain to obtain if she simply accepts Scott's offer, and this is the offer she should statistically make. In other words, it means that the risk is acceptable compared to the potentially significant gain in value she would achieve if it was accepted. But, of course, $4,800 is just a probabilistic expected value that she will never obtain. The reality is that Ann will actually secure a bonus of $3,000 if she accepts Scott's offer, $6,000 if he accepts her new offer, or $0 if he walks out of the negotiation and she is left with no agreement at all.

Before making her final decision, Ann needs to first address a few additional questions. How confident is she of her 80 percent estimate? There is always the chance that Scott will turn down Ann's offer. In that case, what will he do? Will he walk out of the negotiation, or will he respond with yet another counteroffer? By addressing these questions and further considering the statistical perspective, this helps Ann refine her judgment and build her self-confidence.

Given these considerations, and her perception of Scott's negotiation style and personality, Ann strongly believed that Scott was highly likely to accept her final offer. Further, she believed that if Scott did not accept her final offer, he would rather make another counteroffer than break the negotiation. Ann therefore decided to make Scott her final offer of $16 with an allowance of $15,000.

Ann was in a BLUE space where it was fairly easy for her to manoeuvre as she reached closure. Let's now consider a scenario in a RED space.

Paul has had a tough sales negotiation with Liz. Despite a pleasant prelude, the meeting became tense after Paul made his introductory offer at $185 per unit for the volume that Liz required. Liz responded by saying that this was totally out of line and indicated that her target was way below that, at just $120.

Over the course of several exchanges, Liz indicated that she was totally uninterested in any sort of allowance and that she just wanted a "fair" price. She was very sober in her communication, inflexible in her pricing requests, and professional but not agreeable. She told Paul that the meeting will soon have to come to an end and that she expects Paul to make his final best offer.

Paul's last offer was at $160, and Liz had not been willing to change her own last offer of $130. Preparing his response, Paul realized that, beyond Liz's personality, there could have been other reasons why they had not been able to converge to a smaller pricing gap. In particular, it could be that his offers were above her BATNA, or even that there was no ZOPA, hence no possibility of an agreement.

Paul knew that he could not match Liz's request at $130 as it was below his own BATNA of $140. Using his sales-support application, Paul observed that $140 would result in a $4,000 bonus for him. He also suspected that this was probably below Liz's BATNA, as she certainly kept some pricing latitude for herself, and he estimated that there was a 90 percent chance she would accept this offer. He also considered the option of making an offer at $150, which would provide him with a bonus of $9,000. However, Paul thought there was only a 50 percent chance that she would accept this higher offer (see Paul's probabilistic choices in Table 10.2).

Table 10.2   Paul's probabilistic choices ($).

	Paul's price	Liz's price	Paul's bonus	Probability of closure (%)
First round	185	120		
Last round	160	130		
Paul's BATNA	140		4,000	90
Paul's option	150		9,000	50

Paul first considered the probabilistic value of these two offers. At $140, he could obtain a $4,000 bonus with a probability of 90 percent, resulting in an expected bonus of $3,600. At $150, he could obtain a much higher $9,000 bonus, but with only a 50 percent probability, resulting in an expected bonus $4,500. Paul evaluated these two expected outcomes to be somewhat equivalent given the uncertainty in his probability estimates.

Paul thus weighed other considerations. If he makes the $150 offer and Liz turns it down, Paul thinks that she is unlikely to make a counteroffer or to ask him to improve it at this point. Given the way the encounter had gone, and Liz's current disposition, it would probably be the end of the meeting and Paul will have achieved nothing for all his efforts. He also realizes that if $150 happens to be above Liz's BATNA, the probability of her accepting is not 50 percent, but it is actually 0 percent. Paul needs to avoid this situation as he has been unlucky in his recent sales negotiations and cannot afford another miss.

At $140, Paul feels more confident in his probability estimate of 90 percent acceptance by Liz. He would have to explain to her how he can now afford to drop his price by $20 while he had been so far making only small, step-by-step price reductions. He thought he could explain this as a major sacrifice to gain her account, at the same time he would congratulate Liz for her tough bargaining. If she made a counteroffer at this point, however, Paul would have reached his BATNA and would have no price slack left. In this case, he knew he could firmly explain that this was his final offer, and he could not improve it.

Paul remembered the old saying, "a bird in the hand is worth two in the bush." Despite having some regrets for letting go of the shinier alternative, he decided to swallow his pride and drop his price significantly—to $140. At least he had the satisfaction of knowing that he was still generating corporate value at that price, and that, while not reaching his objective, he would still obtain some bonus.

The contrasting stories of Ann and Paul illustrate the various facets of risk management when closing for value capture, including assessing probabilities, estimating expected values, considering highest and lowest risk, and anticipating recovery or adjustment options. Hopefully, they have also demonstrated to you that while you cannot always be right in a world of uncertainties, you can improve your odds with a structured approach and some simple techniques. And that it can be fun practicing to improve one's risk-management skills!

Let's now get back to Tom and his meeting with Sue.

Tom Closing

ABC, bridging the gap, BLUE and RED spaces, the closure map, the cliff, managing risk. . .Tom was reminiscing about the session on closure for value capture in the WAWS programme as he prepared to close his encounter with Sue, the professional buyer at MARINTEK. He smiled as he remembered the nickname Sue's people gave her: "the shark." Tom actually thought that his meeting with Sue had gone better than he had anticipated, and he looked forward to closing the deal.

When he went for a break with his coach Claudia, Tom was pleased that he and Sue had managed to reach a point where they had only a $5/unit gap for an order of 11,000 units. He was confident that they were in the BLUE space and that an agreement was almost certain. Tom agreed that he would share with Claudia the reasoning behind his next offer as he prepared for closure.

Using his sales-support application, Tom found that at the $175 price requested by Sue, he was at 132 percent of his corporate-value objective, resulting in a $15,820 bonus for an agreement at that level. At the $180 he was proposing, he could instead generate 136 percent of his corporate-value objective and earn a $16,348 bonus. The differences did not feel significant to Tom, and he thought that his top priority was to obtain closure in the best way possible to preserve a fruitful relationship with Sue and MARINTEK beyond the current transaction. This meant ensuring Sue's satisfaction while at the same time displaying strong negotiation power corresponding to the quality of the E150 and ELTRON's stellar reputation.

Accepting Sue's price request would certainly achieve the first objective, but it could express a too-easy conciliation. In addition, Tom suspected that, while she did not want to consider an allowance at an earlier stage, Sue would probably ask for a substantial one as a last-minute concession. To give her full satisfaction, Tom knew that he would have to accept the last request she would make as opposed to trying to impose his last offer on her.

Tom checked that with a price at $180, he could offer Sue an allowance of $55,000 and generate the same corporate value as with a price of $175 and no allowance. The same would go for Sue's corporate value as well—she would be equally inclined to accept an offer at $175 and no allowance, or an offer at $180 with a $55,000 allowance. Tom suspected, however, that Sue would request a further allowance on top of whatever he proposed. He also thought it was better for future negotiations to give a higher allowance now than to set a lower price precedent.

Consequently, Tom decided to indicate that he could not lower his price below $180, but that he could offer a $60,000 allowance. He decided this should be more valuable to Sue than $175 and no allowance. Expecting that Sue would feel obliged to ask for an additional concession, he decided that he could potentially increase the allowance up to $90,000 if necessary.

Claudia listened to Tom's reasoning and agreed that it made sense. It is with this closure approach in mind that they returned to the meeting room where Sue was waiting for them.

After a short, polite exchange, Tom told Sue that he had carefully looked at what he could do, and while not being able to go for a price below $180, he was willing to make an effort by offering an allowance of $60,000. Sue indicated that she was disappointed that he was not willing to agree to her price demand, but her body language indicated that this was a purely formal protest. She thanked Tom for offering an allowance but that it was somewhat insufficient to make up for the $180 price.

Tom replied that he could not do much better and asked her what she needed to close the deal. Sue indicated that she would find it fair if he increased the allowance to $70,000. Tom expressed a mild protest and indicated that he would have to check the implications on his sales-support application. He, of course, already knew that this was a good resolution. Glancing at his tablet, he confirmed to himself that at $180 a unit, and with a $70,000 allowance, he would reach 131 percent of his corporate-value objective and was well on his way to a bonus of around $15,000 (see Table 10.3, for a comparison of Tom's closure options).

Table 10.3   Tom's closure options ($).

	Price	Allowance	Corporate value (%)	Bonus
Sue's position	175	0	132	15,820
Tom's position	180	0	136	16,348
Tom's options				
Equivalent to Sue's position	180	55,000	132	15,820
Offered to Sue	180	60,000	132	15,550
Counteroffer by Sue	180	70,000	131	15,000

Turning back to Sue, he indicated that he could make this deal work and was happy to be able to accept her request. Sue was delighted at the outcome, and with a large smile and expressive eyes, she gave Tom a firm handshake.

MOVING ON

As they were leaving the MARINTEK premises, Claudia congratulated Tom for his conduct of the negotiation with Sue and the agreement they had reached. Having talked with Sue before the meeting, and knowing her objectives, Claudia knew that the agreement was also a good outcome for Sue. Tom and Claudia decided to go for lunch together to take the opportunity to review and debrief Tom's first value-capture experience since he participated in the WAWS programme.

CHAPTER 11

WIN AND LEARN, LEARN TO WIN

The hunger to win is a great engine of self-development and progress. The British have long been a great sailing nation, and in the 1800s, they raced their huge tea clippers from China to London. Why? Because the first loads of tea to arrive in the new season commanded a higher price. An early example of value capture!

The construction of clippers was continuously improved to win the tea race, culminating in very fast sailing ships like the *Cutty Sark* which can still be seen in Greenwich, close to London. Interestingly, the ship's motto, inscribed on its stern, is "WHERE THERES A WILLIS A WAY"—a bit of wordplay referencing both the famous slogan, "Where there's a will, there's a way," and John Willis, the original owner of the *Cutty Sark*.

In 1851, the Royal Yacht Squadron of Great Britain created the Hundred Guinea Cup for a race around the Isle of Wight. The race was a challenge thrown down by the British to other nations. Unfortunately for them, a schooner from the New York Yacht Club won the race. When Queen Victoria was informed of the winner by a signalman on board the Royal Yacht, she asked which boat had secured second place. The signalman replied, "Ah, Your Majesty, there is no second." This is the true spirit in sports, where winning is really being number one!

This was the only time the Hundred Guinea Cup race was held, and the schooner *America* won it. The cup was brought back to New York and the first America's Cup race took place in 1870—named after the ship that defeated the British. Another example of value capture! The America's Cup has been running regularly ever since and is a constant source of shipbuilding innovations as well as novel sailing strategies and tactics.

Yes, the hunger to win is a great source of self-development and progress!

WIN AND LEARN

Tom had the strong hunger to win that made him an award-winning sales pro. However, he became quite anxious when his company, ELTRON, announced that it would focus more on corporate-value creation. This announcement had numerous implications on the sales force, including a new incentive scheme more complex than the simple commission based on revenues. Tom knew that optimizing his incentives would require more of the kind of financial acumen that he personally lacked. And he knew it would mean shifting his mindset from bigger is better to *richer is better*. The WAWS training programme offered by ELTRON prepared Tom and his colleagues to better face this latest sales transformation, and Claudia's coaching had reassured him.

With his first significant win at MARINTEK, Tom felt confident that he could now succeed in this new value-capture game—just as he had previously done when the focus was on revenue growth.

After the meeting at MARINTEK, Claudia and Tom stopped by a local restaurant for lunch. As a professional sales coach, with previous experience in sports, Claudia knew the importance of debriefing immediately after a sales negotiation. After they took their seats at a table, Claudia asked Tom to give her his impressions of the encounter.

Tom was understandably still very excited about the successful outcome of his meeting with Sue, and he took a moment to recollect his thoughts about what he had done to prepare from the time he had his first contact with MARINTEK. This is what he told Claudia.

In the first selling phase, he built a good relationship with two individuals at MARINTEK, Alan from engineering and Pat from manufacturing. Building these relationships was key to getting the E150 approved by the company and moving to the second selling phase, negotiating an agreement with Sue. He was glad that Alan had mentioned Sue's nickname—"the shark"—in passing. This alerted Tom to the fact that he had better be well prepared for his negotiation with her, which included reviewing his notes from the WAWS programme.

Tom had learned about MARINTEK's business during his discussions with Alan and Pat, but he did some additional research to further his knowledge. He framed his mission carefully, understanding how the negotiating variables of volume, price, and allowance influenced the creation of corporate value, and hence his bonus. From this, Tom developed his BATNA frontier and analyzed it to understand the implications.

He next attempted to anticipate Sue's BATNA frontier, recalling that this was the most difficult part of preparing for a sales negotiation. But he liked the way this helped him come up with a variety of different alternatives for what Sue's procurement approach might be. Tom was pleased to have realized that she would probably have a different attitude toward secondary suppliers than toward a primary supplier. Overlaying Sue's anticipated BATNA frontier with his own, Tom determined that there was a ZOPA, and he then explored the options that it offered. He designed a strategy to make an opening offer at $200 for 11,000 units with an objective of $190 for 10,000 units.

At the beginning of the encounter, Tom felt that he and Sue had a good and pleasant exchange. When Sue mentioned a need for 20,000 units, the high end of the bracket mentioned by Pat, he knew that she was the type to exaggerate her requirements. He remembers having been surprised when Sue made the first move and planted her pricing anchor at $160 per unit for "large volumes" without being specific about what that meant. He was satisfied not to have been impressed by this unexpected move and to have maintained his opening price at $200, but for a higher volume of 12,000 units.

Despite Sue's strong reaction and resistance to making a counteroffer, Tom did not weaken his position, and he was able to establish his credibility as a negotiator while gaining Sue's respect. Throughout the entire bargaining session, Tom actively listened to Sue and carefully observed her body language. He believed he had made a positive move when he proposed reducing his volume ambitions to 8,000 units, resulting in a protest from Sue. He interpreted this protest as a tip-off that she was considering making ELTRON her main supplier.

Tom then responded to Sue's hints, moving the discussion to 11,000 units. The small price gap they reached after a number of bargaining moves was a relief. Tom observed that he had decreased his price from $200 to $180, while Sue had increased the price she demanded from only $170 to $175. This disparity must have given Sue a great sense of satisfaction even though it was—unknown to her—right in line with Tom's strategy and that it would potentially generate significant corporate value for his company.

Tom was also happy about the analysis he did during the break he and Sue took toward the end of the negotiation meeting. Being firm on his $180 price with a generous allowance gave Sue a better total offer than she had expected. Tom also anticipated Sue's final request for an increase of the allowance. Granting this request would allow him to maintain a good relationship with Sue for future transactions and establish his credibility as a professional partner.

Claudia had carefully listened to Tom's recollections, remaining silent but occasionally nodding her head to show her approval. She also smiled to indicate her happiness in sharing Tom's success.

When Tom was done sharing his story, he was so enthusiastic that Claudia did not want to spoil his mood by asking him what he could have done better—a classic question in her coaching practice. Instead, she congratulated him for his success and clear reasoning throughout the entire process. She volunteered to write up a debrief summary to review with Tom, and he was excited to get the results.

Claudia took out her notebook—she had filled many pages with her writing as she listened to Tom and Sue talk through the expectations they had for their pending negotiation. However, Claudia tore out just one page from the notebook, and on this page she had listed seven headings followed by a single-word rating:

- Corporate value mastery: Excellent
- Steering customer satisfaction: Excellent
- Leadership attitude: Excellent
- Preparation: Great
- Strategy: Excellent
- Tactics: Great
- Closure: Excellent

After Tom read through the ratings, Claudia elaborated on what she had observed about his performance for each of the seven headings, repeatedly complimenting him. She summarized her observations by telling Tom that he had applied, with his own style, the key principles of value capture as taught in the WAWS programme. She was delighted that, in addition to being the excellent *value-creation* sales pro he already was, he now had everything he needed to be an excellent *value-capture* sales pro.

Tom had listened intently and enjoyed this short summary of what had taken place during his encounter with Sue. When Claudia finished her debrief, Tom could not help but ask her why she had noted "Excellent" for each heading except for preparation and tactics, which she had rated as "Great."

Claudia smiled. She had expected this question but did not want to elaborate unless Tom asked. Claudia told Tom that these were the two areas where she thought he had some opportunities for improvement. Under preparation, she repeated that Tom had done a great job but noted that he missed an opportunity.

More specifically, when Alan and Pat jokingly called Sue "the shark," Tom could have engaged in an informal conversation with them to find out more about Sue to be better prepared for his encounter with her. Alan and Pat had developed a good relationship with Tom, and they approved the ELTRON E150 because they thought it was a superior product. Whatever supplier Sue ultimately negotiated an agreement with, it was Alan and Pat who would have to live with the consequences of this decision, not Sue. They therefore had a vested interest in that decision being the right one.

Having approved the E150, they became internal advocates for the product. This is why they warned Tom about "the shark." It would have been worthwhile for Tom to take a moment to ask them to expand further, without obviously divulging any company secrets. Tom could have learned more about Sue's personality and how best to interact with her.

As Claudia explained her reasoning, Tom's eyes lit up. He had indeed been intrigued that they had volunteered Sue's nickname, and now realized it may have been an invitation to exchange further. With the rush at the end of his conversation with Alan and Pat, he hesitated to ask them to tell him more. But after talking with Claudia, he realized that it would have taken only a few minutes of their time, and the information he gained would have been valuable. Tom pledged to himself that he would be more attentive to such opportunities to gain information like this in the future.

Claudia then moved to the other item with a less-than-excellent rating: tactics. She started by telling Tom that he did a great job in his bargaining session with Sue, and that the outcome was more than satisfactory in all three dimensions of value capture: profitability, market share, and customer satisfaction. Tom was in fact at more than 130 percent of the objective. There was just a small possible improvement that was usually difficult to see, but that could help Tom in his future negotiations.

Claudia reminded Tom that she also had a preparatory session with Sue before the sales negotiation started. During this session, Sue revealed her procurement approach to Claudia with the understanding that it would remain confidential until after the end of the negotiations. The objective was to provide some information usually not available, but which would benefit both Tom and Sue when they were debriefed afterward by Claudia.

This is what Sue told Claudia: "I have simple negotiating instructions for this product category. I must initially secure a supply of 16,000 units, an amount that will eventually be adjusted over the year. We ideally want to have a total of three to four suppliers. We would like to have a privileged partner, covering from 50 to 70 percent of our needs. We expect this primary partner to give us a highly competitive price based on a guaranteed volume. Of course, if all goes well, we anticipate maintaining a stable, long-term relationship with this supplier."

Sue continued. "We expect any supplier to provide this product at a price below \$280/unit for volumes up to 3,000 units. This price will allow us to cover our costs and make a modest margin. We do not want to squeeze the price from secondary suppliers too hard as we want to protect their existence to offer variety, a stable source of supply, and bargaining power. On the other hand, we expect our primary supplier to give us a discount of at least \$10/unit per extra 1,000 units above 3,000. It is from the primary supplier that we really make the bulk of our profit."

"These are the maximum prices we aim at," Sue told Claudia, "but of course my incentive is to obtain the lowest prices possible, while ensuring that we get the quality that we require. We could maybe have a price as low as \$120 for our total volume of 16,000 units. It is, however, unlikely that we could find a supplier at such a low price, and we would probably resist being so dependent on a single supplier anyway. In any case, we will also negotiate an extra allowance from all our suppliers. We do not have a real norm on this. Frankly, we always try to get as much as we can. It all depends on the price offered, but usually the allowance is more an extra in case the price is still too high, and not a deal breaker if the price is right."

Tom's eyes were wide open as he could now better understand Sue's behaviour. She had hidden her cards pretty well to the end, and he felt even better to have manoeuvred the way he did during the bargaining and at closure.

Claudia then showed Tom a graph she had prepared for the debrief (Figure 11.1). It illustrated Tom's BATNA frontier as well as two BATNA frontiers for Sue—the one expected by Tom and the real one revealed by Sue.

Claudia pointed out to Tom that while the general procurement principles anticipated by Tom were correct—for example, a more-favourable treatment of secondary suppliers—Sue's real BATNA frontier was above the one expected by Tom for volumes higher than 9,000 units. This meant that above this level, Sue was less demanding than Tom had expected. Claudia then showed Tom that the final agreement, marked by a cross on Figure 11.1, was on the BATNA frontier that Tom had anticipated for Sue, but about $20 below Sue's real BATNA frontier.

This was in itself quite an achievement for Tom and a reward for his strategy. However, Tom could have negotiated a higher price for this volume or obtained a higher volume for the same price. Claudia then observed that this is the reason why Sue had signaled, with too much subtlety maybe, that she wanted to explore higher volumes.

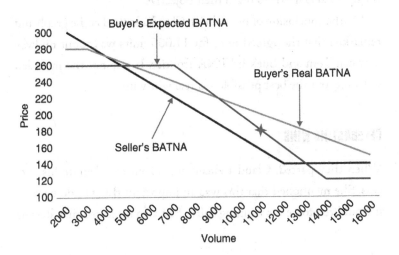

Figure 11.1   Buyer's BATNA, expected vs. real.

Claudia also remarked that Tom was probably focused so much on his strategy, based on the BATNA frontier he had anticipated for Sue, that he did not pick up her signals and update his strategy accordingly. She said this was a classic mistake of holding too closely to one's predefined strategy despite receiving new signals. A value-capture strategy is indeed essential to prepare for a sales negotiation, but it should not be cast in stone. One should not hesitate to update it in real time as new insights emerge.

Claudia continued her debrief, telling Tom that he had displayed a model application of the principles in the WAWS programme. According to Claudia, this was even more important for Tom's future performance than the excellent outcome he had achieved that day. This first sales meeting after the programme, where Claudia could have a confidential conversation with the buyer and discover her BATNA, was a unique opportunity. In his future sales negotiations, Tom should be happy to reach the most valuable agreements he could negotiate, with the knowledge that he could always have obtained better, without knowing how much. This is normal since the buyer also needs to reach their objective.

At the conclusion of her debrief, Claudia looked at the graph and remarked that the agreed price for 11,000 units was about midway between Tom and Sue's BATNA frontier. It was not the intended outcome, but the best possible—a real win-win!

CELEBRATING WINS

When they parted, Claudia encouraged Tom to celebrate his success. She mentioned that this was an important thing to do because it would reinforce his winning spirit. She also indicated that sharing with others what happened, factually and without arrogance, would not only help others to learn from his experience but would also give him opportunities to reflect further.

Of course, the first person to learn about Tom's success was his wife, Lola. She had witnessed how anxious her husband had been when ELTRON announced that they were focusing more on corporate-value creation and transforming their sales incentives accordingly. Lola was not knowledgeable about sales, but as a financial analyst at a bank, she could understand value capture and negotiations. She listened attentively to Tom's account of the encounter with Sue and the debriefing with Claudia, asking several pertinent questions that induced Tom to revisit some aspects of his strategy and tactics.

In the days that followed, Tom happily shared his MARINTEK experience with his boss and colleagues. They heartily congratulated him—discussing different aspects of the value-capture negotiation, including the debriefing with Claudia. Tom waited a week before contacting Alan and Pat—he wanted Sue to have the first opportunity to inform them about the agreement. They were delighted for Tom, but they were also happy because a significant portion of the boats for the new model year would be equipped with the E150. Tom assured them that they would get great service from his ELTRON colleagues as MARINTEK implemented the E150 into their manufacturing process. They both expressed their pleasure in having the opportunity to work together with Tom in the future.

A few weeks later, Tom received an updated version of the dashboard for his MARINTEK agreement on his sales support application (Figure 11.2).

Figure 11.2   Tom's dashboard for the MARINTEK agreement.

Right away, Tom noticed the 85 percent score for customer satisfaction. This was the rating Sue gave to the agency consulting with
her after the agreement was signed with Tom. She was really pleased
with the interaction she had with Tom and the resulting agreement.
This augured well for the future of their business relationship and
additional orders for the next year. And it helped boost the corporate value generated by this agreement to 135 percent of the objective, with the same impact on Tom's bonus. This outcome was truly
something to celebrate with his family!

LEARNING TO WIN

Tom had previously learned what it takes to become a top sales
professional, creating value for his offers in the mind of customers,
closing sales, and earning a good income on commissions based on
revenues. He had become a winner at this game—attending sales
seminars, reading the latest books on the topic, searching the internet for new approaches and techniques, kicking around selling ideas

with colleagues, and more. He had also improved his skills through his own experience, recognizing especially how the diversity of clients and selling situations helped him explore, test, and refine new approaches.

Adapting to a new selling mission focused on corporate value—with multiple objectives, new incentives, and the requirement for greater business acumen—could have been a big hurdle for Tom. Fortunately, the WAWS programme offered by his company helped him and his colleagues cross the troubled waters of change and reach the other bank to start their new journey through the 3rd sales transformation.

Each of us has the ability to learn by ourselves, continuously improving the skills that we have already mastered. But when facing a new challenge, we can learn faster if we receive some help from others. This was the purpose of the WAWS programme offered at ELTRON, and indeed the purpose of this book on value-capture selling.

Allocating time to learn is a personal investment to be more effective in the future. Remember the "sharpening the saw" parable in Chapter 6? This was the story of an exhausted woodcutter who justified his ineffective approach by saying, "I don't have time to sharpen the saw. I'm too busy sawing!" At the time, I mentioned this parable to encourage you to develop your leadership as your role in the 3rd sales transformation has been expanded to create corporate value rather than to just bring in revenues. The same is equally valid when it comes to developing your specific skills for value capture.

Learning by reading a book or an internet post, by listening to a lecture or podcast, or by participating in a webinar, are all examples of what is called *formal learning*. It is, however, only one way to learn, and not the most important.

Experts in the field of learning and development (L&D) often refer to the 70-20-10 model, which is based on research pursued by the Center for Creative Leadership in the 1990s.[1] This model provides an indication of the three ways in which learning and development take place in a business context. The greatest proportion, 70 percent, comes from your own experience. This is called *experiential learning*. Then 20 percent comes from being challenged by others. This is called *social learning*. The smallest proportion, just 10 percent, occurs through *formal learning*.

This doesn't mean that every individual learns in this specific, 70-20-10 way, in every learning situation. But it is useful as a guide to emphasize that the learning required to achieve high performance in business situations happens primarily through experience and being challenged by others.

This also doesn't mean that the relatively small amount of learning and development that occurs through formal learning is useless. Quite the opposite, because formal learning is an accelerator for the other two forms of learning. What you learned in this book should help you learn further as you apply the principles in your practice and gain more from your future experience.

With the formal learning side of value capture being well covered by this book, I will now give you my best advice on social and experiential learning so that you can further develop your value-capture abilities and be a winner in the 3rd sales transformation.

SOCIAL LEARNING TO WIN

For social learning, the easiest, fastest, and most advantageous way is to have one or more challenging partners with whom you can openly exchange your experience, successes, failures, and doubts. They can be trusted colleagues at work, or they can be friends or family.

You could obviously think of your boss as a challenging partner, although this is feasible only in the case of the still somewhat exceptional bosses who are self-confident, have created a learning culture in their team, and see mentoring as part of their role. This is indeed the trend in leadership today, and managers are being trained and encouraged to leave behind traditional "bossy" practices and develop their teams for high performance. It is for you to assess what type of boss you have and how much you can comfortably share with them. In any case, it is better to start with colleagues or friends.

But even then, some sales professionals find this exercise difficult to jump into the first time. I remember Sofia, an experienced and successful salesperson, who was receiving good feedback from her manager. Despite her enviable record, she obviously did not succeed in everything she did. But being a high achiever, she wanted to continue to improve her skills.

In a seminar, Sofia confided to me some of the difficulties she had encountered and what she thought were personal failures. I listened attentively to her, asked a few questions, and pointed to a couple potential improvements she could make. Sofia was happy to discover that in just a short time, new doors had been opened that she could explore further for her self-improvement.

I then asked Sofia if she had previously shared with anyone what she had just told me. She appeared surprised by the question and said, "No." I asked her why not, and she became visibly uncomfortable. I encouraged her to think about it and we agreed that we would together create a short list of reasons for her not having done so.

Soon, a list of reasons emerged, including such things as uncertainty in the value of the approach, difficulty in finding a competent partner, the question of why anybody would spend the time to help her, lack of trust in some colleagues, and vulnerability in sharing potential errors or weaknesses. We went through the list and agreed that all these reasons were valid concerns, justifying a careful selection of a challenging partner.

I advised Sofia to start openly sharing her doubts with different people she could trust, beginning with some innocuous issues. This would serve as a test of their willingness and ability to constructively challenge her. She could then offer reciprocity to develop a strong, long-term relationship with a selected business sparring partner. Sofia could see all the development benefits she could gain from such a win-win, balanced partnership, and she wished she had engaged in this process earlier.

The rewards that come from having a trusted, long-term challenging partner are beyond what one can project. The principle is that we often have tunnel vision or bias in situations, depending on what it is we want to prove or obtain. That means that we naturally tend to look at evidence that supports our point of view and neglects other aspects—giving it greater weight. There are blind spots in our vision.

The notion of *devil's advocate* expresses well the role of a challenging partner. The term was formalized in 1587 by the Roman Catholic Pope Sixtus V to avoid biased consensual agreement when considering the canonization of an individual to sainthood. It consisted in naming one person—the *advocatus diaboli*, Latin for *devil's advocate*—who was charged with gathering the arguments opposing the decision proposed by the majority. The challenging partners need to be critical, so it's important to entertain a strong, open, and trustworthy relationship with them.

The second way to foster your social learning is to have a coach. The role of coaches is different from the role of challenging partners. In particular, whether professional or benevolent, coaches need to possess strong empathy and specialized skills.

Remember the way Claudia coached Tom in their interactions? She first encouraged Tom, let him take the initiative, asked him carefully selected questions, encouraged him to develop his rationale, and listened actively. When it came time for the debrief, Claudia first commended Tom on the strong points of his negotiation with Sue. She took lots of notes and could have then gone into a more critical examination of Tom's performance, just as a professor would do with a student assignment. But this would not have been coaching.

The role of a coach is not to evaluate an individual's performance, but to help an individual improve their performance. This requires being sensitive to the situation of the individual, their capacity to absorb guidance, and the value of that guidance for future performance. At Tom's invitation, Claudia identified just two specific areas for improvement that he could easily follow and practice in his future sales meetings. She had evaluated that these were the two most-valuable areas for Tom to focus on, that he could handle them fruitfully, but that she should not go further.

Having a coach is a great approach for accelerating learning and performance. Contrary to challenging partners, you should not aim to have access to a coach on a permanent basis. Coaches can be really valuable for a period of 6–12 months when you are facing a new, important challenge. Getting a coach is something you can negotiate with your firm, or you may need to ask someone you know and trust who has coaching experience to effectively play this role for you.

EXPERIENTIAL LEARNING TO WIN

For the part of the 70-20-10 model with the greatest weight, experiential learning, the most obvious way to further improve your performance is to apply the insights you absorbed from the social learning and formal learning components into your practice. Once you have done that, you can then test your understanding of them, their relevance, and their impact.

When trying to apply something we just learned and comprehended, it's often a surprise to us when we realize we have not actually fully understood it as we put it into practice. The most obvious examples of this come from sports, and especially golf. The instructor gives you some advice on how to improve a specific aspect of your game—let's say, a 100-foot pitch—and demonstrates it a couple of times. It looks simple and you are certain you comprehend it fully.

However, before you have your next golf outing with clients, you decide to first try the new technique on the practice range. Only at this moment will you know if you have actually mastered the advice the instructor gave you, or if you need more hints!

The same is true in business. Taking the time to practice any insights you have gained—for example, the ones you have taken from this book on value capture—before applying them in a real negotiation will surely contribute to your self-development and performance. There are two ways to develop your experiential learning on value capture that I advise you to take before going into a real sales negotiation.

The first is role-playing. This is a classic exercise in negotiation workshops of all types, but it is particularly easy to implement by practicing your value-capture skills with a friend. For instance, decide that you will play the role of Emma, the seller, and your friend, Stan, will play the role of the buyer.

First, agree on a list price, let's say $30, and a volume range, let's say up to 5,000 units. Then, as Emma, you will secretly define her commercial guidelines. This will determine Emma's BATNA frontier and her unit cost, while helping her compute the profitability of a deal. On his side, Stan will secretly define the procurement guide-lines that will determine his own BATNA frontier, as well as the price at which he expects to resell the product to determine his prof-itability of a deal.

To keep it simple, consider that each party must maximize their profitability—consideration of other drivers of corporate value would require some additional computational support. Just setting up the context of the game will help both of you better understand the variety of starting conditions in which you can find yourself, from a weak to a strong negotiating position.

As you play your negotiation game, you will be able to practice all the techniques presented in this book, including defining a strat-egy, obtaining insights from the prelude, exploring the existence of a ZOPA, bargaining toward a position favourable for you, identify-ing if you are converging toward a BLUE space or getting stuck in a RED one, and attempting to close a good agreement.

As you finish a game, you can "put your cards on the table" and check with Stan to see if there was a ZOPA, how your bargaining evolved all the way to closure, and discuss how you could have done better. It is also a good idea to change roles as buyer and seller to see the situation from the other side of the fence.

You can start initially with a completely fictitious game and then organize a role-play based on your own data before starting a real negotiation, with a friend taking on the role of the buyer you will eventually meet. As you can imagine, the variety of situations and learning possibilities of role-play for value capture are limitless.

The second experiential learning approach I advise is the use of a computerized value-capture simulator. The approach is like the role-plays described above except that you play the role of a seller against virtual buyers simulated in a software application. This approach offers a number of advantages. One obvious advantage is the dramatically increased computational power available to you, which allows consideration of multiple negotiation variables and corporate-value drivers, which is not possible in a simple role-play. And with this computational power comes increased speed of feedback which favours learning.

Another feature of a simulator is the replicability of a value-capture experience. You can repeat a negotiation with the same virtual buyer multiple times and analyze the impact of different strategies and tactics. With a change in parameters, a simulator can also provide a systematic diversity of negotiating situations.

Finally, a large number of individuals can play the role of sellers in front of exactly the same simulated buyer, allowing a benchmarking of value-capture experiences.

These four characteristics—computational power, replicability, diversity, and benchmarking—make a simulator a particularly effective tool for experiential learning of value capture. The REV-MANEX simulator has been developed to provide a general experiential learning platform for value capture. It may also be worthwhile in some cases to develop value-capture simulators customized for specific situations.

WINNING AND LEARNING TRAPS

Continuous learning is the key to self-development, increased performance, and winning over the challenges you will face in the future. Some people enjoy learning, others find it a chore. In my view, our attitudes about learning come mainly from our personal experiences with it at a young age—experiences that we carry with us for the rest of our life.

If you know people who find learning new things to be a chore, the best gift you can give them is to put them in situations where they will enjoy learning. A good approach is to create playful situations in which they can have fun and acquire new insights, seeing for themselves the value of being happier or more successful.

Having a positive attitude is indeed the first determinant driver of success, and this is why I gave Chapter 6 the title, "The Leadership *Attitude*." Given that you've got the proper attitude, the main hurdle to learning is a lack of time, as indicated by the "sharpening the saw" parable. Learning is an investment of time for a benefit that will be visible only in the future. Other activities compete with our time, and these activities are often more urgent or offer an immediate reward. This is why learning happens if we consciously make time for it and also obtain an immediate reward—the enjoyment of acquiring new insights.

When someone has the proper attitude and allocates the required time, they need one more thing: access to learning tools. This is exactly why I have exposed you to the tools that I believe are the most appropriate for learning and increasing your performance in value-capture selling, throughout the entire 70-20-10 range.

Once you have attitude, time, and tools, you have all the ingredients required for successful self-development and winning at the value-capture selling game. But increasing your performance over time involves a personal journey during which you will encounter many hurdles and traps, any of which have the potential to slow you down or even force you to a standstill.

The main trap against learning and winning is what is called attribution. The concept of attribution theory has long been developed in psychology and has since been the subject of many studies.[2] Its originator, psychologist Fritz Heider, determined that the way people feel and relate to others was largely determined by the way they attribute the results of their actions, especially in terms of external or internal factors:

- **External attribution.** When the cause of an outcome is attributed to an external factor—it is outside of your control. Examples include the weather, the state of the economy, your competitors, your colleagues, and so on. You cannot be held responsible for these causes.
- **Internal attribution.** When the cause of an outcome is attributed to an internal factor—it is within your control. Examples include the decisions you make, your actions, your skills, your communication, and more. You should feel personally responsible for these causes.

Attribution theory has been used by psychologists to investigate what drives human behaviour. Let's consider a simple example.

You enter a store and meet an angry salesperson with the name Hazel displayed on her badge. Before you interact with this person, it might be a good idea to first ask yourself why she is angry. Is it because she is naturally bad-tempered (an internal cause) or because she happens to have had a problem at work or in her personal life (an external cause)? Depending on the attribution of this anger, you should tailor the way you respond to her. To gauge this, you could ask Hazel why she feels the way she does before asking her to assist you with a purchase you need to make.

Attribution is thus a valuable tool for you to diagnose the behaviour of others while improving your own interpersonal relations. But the trap in learning and winning is when you make erroneous attributions to the outcome of your own actions, that is, when you attribute the wrong causes to the results that you observed.

The main attribution trap is what psychologists call the *self-serving bias*. This means that human beings are not totally objective when considering the causes of the outcome of an action they are personally responsible for. They tend to give themselves more of the credit when results are positive (an internal attribution) and blame other causes—including bad luck or other people—when the results are negative (an external attribution). For example, if you failed to reach an agreement, you could blame the behaviour of the buyer for this failure as opposed to putting the blame on your own lack of preparation, or your erratic behaviour during the encounter.

Now, don't feel too guilty if you realize that you have exercised this self-serving bias from time to time. Indeed, blaming an external cause is perhaps the best way to remove the pain we feel when we experience failure, and we *all* experience failure—even the top sales pros among us. The self-serving bias is a natural part of the way our brains work, and it has played a vital role in the survival of the human species—maintaining our self-confidence and stamina through difficult times. In fact, if you had the reverse bias—blaming *yourself* for every negative outcome and failure, including from external causes—you would certainly be in a near-constant state of despair and depression.

While the self-serving bias has its advantages, it has also a few problems. One of these problems is that it is a trap against learning and winning. In particular, experiential learning requires that you take time to objectively debrief the causes of a certain outcome.

If the result is positive, and you simply conclude that everything you did was right, you are not learning much for the next challenge. If the outcome is negative, and you blame the situation, somebody else, or bad luck for this outcome, you are not doing anything positive to help yourself learn either.

As explained by John Maxwell, in his book, *Sometimes You Win—Sometimes You Learn*,[3] it is when you fail that the opportunities to learn are at their greatest. I love this book's title, which expresses well the positive spirit of winners, accepting the failures in our lives as golden opportunities to learn. The book's subtitle, "Life's Greatest Lessons Are Gained from Our Losses," plainly indicates the importance of facing losses as learning opportunities, and the book provides a clear approach to learn effectively from failures.

To take the initiative to reflect objectively on a loss, you must first avoid taking the easy way out of blaming it on external factors. This is a real trap. But, equally important, you should take the initiative to reflect objectively on the real causes of a win, and for that you must first avoid the easy way out of believing that you did all the right things.

The self-serving bias works both ways and it is therefore a double trap, and the biggest hurdle to learning and winning. You can avoid falling into this trap by engaging in a systematic debrief, alone or with a coach, after every value-capture negotiation. And do not hesitate to make my personal motto your own: "Win sometimes, learn always."

Make Yourself Lucky

"Luck" is often an external attribution we apply to explain the success of others. As the author, Jean Cocteau, once said "We must believe in luck. For how else can we explain the success of those we don't like?"[4]

In my workshops, one of the engaging exercises I like to present is a short list of business entrepreneurs who have been very successful and achieved fame. I sometimes change the list for different occasions, but it has included Jeff Bezos, Richard Branson, Larry Ellison, Meg Whitman, Bill Gates, Jack Ma, Oprah Winfrey, Elon Musk, Larry Page, Mark Zuckerberg, and other business luminaries.

As part of this exercise, I ask the workshop participants to list three major causes for the success of these businesspeople. Invariably, there is always a group of participants, often over 50 percent, who list *luck* as one of the three factors. And when I ask what they mean by luck, the most-often-mentioned response is that "they were lucky to be at the right place at the right time."

This response is an example of self-serving bias, when we attribute an external factor for someone's success. It is based on an obvious observation that if each of these individuals were born 10 years earlier or 10 years later, they might not have been as successful as they were. But the fallacy of this observation is that many people were there at the same place at the same time who did *not* have the same success.

And when we further investigate the history of these famous entrepreneurs, we will quickly find that each had enormous personal qualities that explain in great part their success, some of them specific to their situation and some of them generalizable. In the latter category, we can find many qualities that drove the ultimate success of these individuals, including vision, passion, energy, people leadership, innovative and competitive spirit, continuous adaptation, resilience, hard work, and more.

Illustrious people from all ages and horizons have found the need to explain with some humour the source of their luck. Here are some pertinent quotations:[5]

- "Luck is what happens when preparation meets opportunity."
- "Chance favours the prepared mind."
- "Diligence is the mother of good luck."
- "I'm a great believer in luck, and I find the harder I work the more I have of it."
- "The more I practise, the luckier I get."

Based on these examples and quotations, what appears to be luck to others seems to most often be the result of skill, preparation, and application.[6]

I often end my workshops suggesting to participants that they practise carefully what I have identified as the four key success factors for business entrepreneurs in any kind of company, in every industry, anywhere in the world:

- Enjoy
- Learn
- Perform
- Be lucky

Enjoy, because if you enjoy what you do, you will always have great energy and immediate rewards. Enjoyment of one's work is better in my view than passion, which can make you blind to some realities.

Learn because, as we have seen earlier, this is the engine of self-development and progress.

Perform because this is how your success will be measured. With the right skills, enjoyment, and learning, you will perform with ease.

Be lucky because if you enjoy, learn, and perform, you will deserve to appear lucky to others as you achieve all the success in business and life that you could ever desire.

In closing this book, I can only give you my best wishes to enjoy, learn, perform, and be lucky at value-capture selling, to make the shift from a bigger is better mindset to a *richer is better mindset*, and to be a winner in the 3rd sales transformation!

EPILOGUE
NEXT STEPS

While we have reached the end of this book, your value-capture story is just beginning. My aim in writing this book was to ensure your personal journey to win the 3rd sales transformation gets off to a great start. And while there may one day be a 4th sales transformation, I don't currently anticipate one, nor do any of the experts in my network. So, we must expect for the foreseeable future that we will continue to face a world of increasingly stronger competition, which means the importance of value capture will only increase.

The value-capture story is *your* story, and it is far from being over. This is why my personal preference is to conclude this book with the next steps that you may take to benefit most from the time you have invested in reading it.

If you enjoyed this book and can relate to the lessons within, make it your close companion until you master them and move on. Truth be told, far too many of the books people buy each year are read only in part, or not read at all, and are condemned to live a lonely life stuck on a shelf or hidden away in a drawer. In terms of price, books are inexpensive compared to other personal development tools available to you. The true cost is the time you spend reading them. I am certain that the benefits you receive from this book will far exceed the cost of the time you spent reading it.

If you want to capture the entirety of this book's value, then make it your own. Highlight parts that catch your interest, scribble notes on it, fold the corners of the pages you want to come back to.

Do not be afraid to damage the book in so doing—one day it will in any case end up in a waste bin. Will this hurt my feelings as an author? Certainly not, because I know the true value of this book comes only from how much benefit you gain from it, and not from its retail price or where it will end up.

The next step, if you can set aside some time to create the opportunity, is to run a workshop for your colleagues or friends—your fellow sales pros—using the contents of this book that you find most appropriate. This can be just for an hour or two, or for one or two days. Explaining or discussing a subject with others is a great way to make sure that you have really understood the topic and then to take it further. If you want to make this workshop livelier and more interactive, you can use the REVMANEX simulator specifically designed for this topic or create your own role-playing exercises using the stories in the book.

If you are attentive, you will also find that you constantly face situations of value capture outside of selling—obviously as a consumer, but also in any situation where you experience conflict with someone else, and even in many peaceful personal discussions. In every one of these situations, you can practise the principles in this book and improve your mastery of value capture.

Selling is an immensely fascinating and rewarding profession. You may, however, move out of sales as you progress in your career, move up the organizational ladder, or change jobs entirely. You might even be hired as a professional buyer to display your skills on the other side of the fence!

The world is full of opportunities. To succeed in exploiting any of them, you will first have to create value but then you will have to capture a share of the value that you have created. That is the very essence of the message I have provided to you in this book.

May this book help you find the success you so richly deserve, while having fun and being happy! I wish you well on your value-capture journey.

THANK YOU, DEAR READER

If you found *Value Capture Selling* valuable for your personal development, please take the time to make it known on Amazon or your favourite social media!

I will be happy to thank you by providing you free access to unlimited practice sessions on the REVMANEX simulator with Mark Swat, the super salesperson. This will allow you to implement some of the techniques in this book and to test your value-capture skills.

Just send a link or a screenshot of your review, blog, or post to licensing@stratxsim.com. StratX Simulations will give you access to a REVMANEX practice session with Mark, as well as a thank-you note from me.

To learn more about the REVMANEX simulator, just scan this QR code:

If you are an instructor and want to use the REVMANEX simulator in your classes or workshops, please contact licensing@stratxsim.com to obtain a licence, or participate in a certification session.

Thank you for reading and recommending *Value Capture Selling*.

ACKNOWLEDGEMENTS

O ver the several years of practice, consulting, and teaching during which time this book has developed and matured, I have benefited immensely from the contributions of my colleagues, clients, and students. My sincere gratitude goes to all of them. Unfortunately, I cannot name every person who has influenced my work in writing this book on value-capture selling, but I would like to recognize a few people in particular.

My first thanks must go to those who took the time out of their busy schedules to review the manuscript in various stages and who made valuable comments, especially (in alphabetical order): Laurent Beraza, Virginie Bodescot, Anna Campagna, Frank Cespedes, Philippe Chiappinelli, Enrico D'Aiuto, Haisen Ding, Dominique Ferrier, Gerhard Gschwandtner, Omar Haddadeen, Gráinne Maycock, Amy Nankervis, Tolga Pekel, Dominique Rouzies, Manish Kumar Singh, Giulia Stefani, Fabio Villanova, Alessandra Vizza and Spencer Wixon.

Many thanks must also go to my colleagues at StratX Simulations who have shared my enthusiasm and contributed to the implementation of the REVMANEX simulator for value-capture selling. Special appreciation to Ali Oulhaci, who directed the software development, and to all those who participated in its testing and deployment.

Many thanks to all those at Wiley who organized the publication of this book with great expertise, and especially Annie Knight, Richard Samson, Susan Cerra, and Gajalakshmi Sivakumar.

My gratitude goes to Peter Economy, whose journalistic talents, great humour, and positive spirit greatly contributed in making this book more accessible and pleasant to read.

And, finally, this book is dedicated to my children, Sylvie and Philippe, and all family members of the next generation, Karine, Valerie, Alex, Caroline, Lucie, Elena, Gaspard, and Felix. May this work, even in a modest way, help them live in a better world where customers, employees, and other business-community stakeholders can work together and prosper in harmony.

ABOUT THE AUTHOR

Jean-Claude ("JC") Larreche is a leading authority on the creation of profitable business growth through value-capture selling, marketing excellence, and customer centricity. Sales pros in every industry, all around the world, have developed their strategic skills by applying Larreche's powerful principles and advice.

He is the author or co-author of many articles and books devoted to continuously raising the bar for the science and practice of sales and marketing, including his bestselling book, *The Momentum Effect*. JC has also designed numerous business simulations and his world-renowned MARKSTRAT has been used successfully by more than a million executives worldwide to develop and sharpen their marketing strategy skills.

Larreche is emeritus professor at INSEAD, the leading international business school with campuses in France, Singapore, and Abu Dhabi. In addition to his distinguished academic career, he has been a consultant for many leading global corporations and served on the board of several companies. He is also the Founding Chairman of StratX Simulations, a leading provider of experiential learning business simulations, with offices in Paris and Boston.

In addition to earning his MBA from INSEAD, JC Larreche received an MSc in Computer Sciences from the University of London and a PhD in Business from Stanford University. It was at Stanford that he was first nicknamed "JC" by his American friends. He currently lives in France but has traveled extensively—working closely with business executives in more than 50 countries.

NOTES

CHAPTER 1

1. For sales management with an emphasis on the importance of strategy, see the two excellent books by Frank V. Cespedes: *Aligning Strategy and Sales: The Choices, Systems, and Behaviors that Drive Effective Selling*, (Boston: HBR Press, 2014), and *Sales Management That Works: How to Sell in a World That Never Stops Changing* (Boston: HBR Press 2021). For a talented analysis of recent changes required in sales management, see Michelle Richardson and Russ Sharer, *Agile and Resilient: Sales Leadership for the New Normal* (Greensboro, NC: The Brooks Group, 2022).
2. Jim Collins, *Good to Great: Why Some Companies Make the Leap and Others Don't* (New York: Harper Business, 2001).
3. The story of Tom at ELTRON and all other examples are inspired by actual people and events. However, they have been designed to provide key principles in a concise and efficient manner. All the names are fictional.

FURTHER SOURCES

"Fifteen Million Salespeople to Be Displaced by 2020, Predicts Sales 2.0 Conference Host," press release, *Business Wire*, March 15, 2011. https://www.businesswire.com/news/home/20110315007164/en/Fifteen-Million-Salespeople-to-Be-Displaced-by-2020-Predicts-Sales-2.0-Conference-Host

"Number of Employed Sales People in the United States in 2020, by Occupation," Statista, September 30, 2022. https://www. statista.com/statistics/960853/number-employed-sales-people-us-occupation/

"The Digital Future of B2B Sales," Roland Berger, May 21, 2016. https://www.rolandberger.com/en/Insights/Publications/The-digital-future-of-B2B-sales-2.html

CHAPTER 2

1. This example was inspired by the case study, "Value Selling at SKF Service," by Kamran Kashani and Aimee DuBrule, IMD-5-0751.
2. See Neil Rackham, *Spin Selling* (New York: McGraw-Hill, 1988).
3. Jill Konrath, *SNAP Selling: Speed Up Sales and Win More Business with Today's Frazzled Customers* (New York: Portfolio, 2012).
4. John Doerr, "RAIN Selling: How to Lead Masterful Sales Conversations," RAIN Group. https://www.rainsalestraining.com/blog/rain-selling-how-to-lead-masterful-sales-conversations
5. Matthew Dixon and Brent Adamson, *The Challenger Sale: Taking Control of the Customer Conversation* (New York: Portfolio Penguin, 2013).
6. Mike Schultz and John Doerr, *Insight Selling: Surprising Research on What Sales Winners Do Differently* (Hoboken, NJ: Wiley, 2014).
7. Jeb Blount, *Fanatical Prospecting: The Ultimate Guide to Opening Sales Conversations and Filling the Pipeline by Leveraging Social Selling, Telephone, Email, Text, and Cold Calling* (Hoboken, NJ: Wiley, 2015).

8. For an excellent book on the importance of understanding emotions in sales, see Jeb Blount, *Sales EQ: How Ultra High Performers Leverage Sales-Specific Emotional Intelligence to Close the Complex Deal* (Hoboken, NJ: Wiley, 2017).

9. Lizzy Knights-Ward, "Moments of Trust: Why Customer Value Is the Key to Sales and Marketing Alignment," LinkedIn (2020), p. 10. https://business.linkedin.com/content/dam/me/business/en-us/marketing-solutions/cx/2020/images/pdfs/moments-of-trust-v4.pdf

10. Philip Kotler, Neil Rackham, and Suj Krishnaswamy, "Ending the War Between Sales and Marketing," *Harvard Business Review*, July–August (2006).

11. Jean-Claude Larreche, *The Momentum Effect: How to Ignite Exceptional Growth* (Harlow: Pearson, 2008).

12. Jonathan Hughes, David Chapnick, Isaac Block, and Saptak Ray, "What Is Customer-Centricity, and Why Does It Matter?" *California Management Review*, September 26, 2021.

13. See for instance the AI-based tools for prospect qualification and value enhancement offered by the new firm Spotlight at HYPERLINK "http://www.spotlight.ai" www.spotlight.ai

FURTHER SOURCES

"Yogurt Worldwide," https://www.statista.com/outlook/cmo/food/dairy-products-eggs/yogurt/worldwide

"5 Biggest Yogurt Companies in the World," https://www.insidermonkey.com/blog/5-biggest-yogurt-companies-in-the-world-918835/4/

"Activia Gut Health Challenge," https://www.activia.us.com/gut-health-challenge/faqs/

CHAPTER 3

1. The evolution of GE from Jack Welch to Larry Culp has been well documented. More information on the facts described here can be found in Mark Jewell, Christopher Rugaber, and Michelle Chapman, "Jack Welch, GE Chief Who Made Bold Acquisition of RCA, NBC, Dies at 84," AP, March 2, 2020. https://www.shootonline.com/news/jack-welch-ge-chief-who-made-bold-acquisition-rca-nbc-dies-84; B. Bentz, M. Seavy-Nesper, and N. Escobar, "Short-Term Profits and Long-Term Consequences—Did Jack Welch Break Capitalism?" *NPR*, June 1, 2022. https://www.npr.org/2022/06/01/1101505691/short-term-profits-and-long-term-consequences-did-jack-welch-break-capitalism; Antoine Gara, "For GE's Jeff Immelt, Hundreds of Deals and $575 Billion Didn't Yield a Higher Stock Price," *Forbes*, June 15, 2017. https://www.forbes.com/sites/antoinegara/2017/06/15/for-ges-jeff-immelt-hundreds-of-deals-and-575-billion-didnt-yield-a-higher-stock-price/

2. The term VUCA originated in *Leaders: Strategies for Taking Charge* by Warren Bennis and Burt Nanus (New York: Harper and Row, 1985). It was first adopted by the US Army and became increasingly used in business.

3. As mentioned earlier, the term *revenue management* is used in some companies to describe this change of emphasis away from plain revenue maximization. It avoids putting upfront the key objective of creating corporate value as this is often misperceived as benefiting only shareholders. Instead of shying away from this actual fact, I prefer to address the issue upfront and communicate that the creation of corporate value is in the interest of all.

FURTHER SOURCES

"Former GE CEO Jack Welch Passes Away at 84," *Mergers and Acquisitions*, March 2, 2020. https://www.themiddlemarket. com/articles/former-ge-ceo-jack-welch-passes-away-at-84

"Jack Welch, The 'Ultimate Manager' Who Oversaw GE's Rise to the Most Valuable Company, Dies at 84," *General Electric*, March 2, 2020. https://www.ge.com/news/reports/jack-welch-the-ultimate-manager-who-oversaw-ges-rise-to-the-most-valuable-company-dies-at-84

"Jeffrey R. Immelt, 1956–," *Reference for Business*, ND. https:// www.referenceforbusiness.com/biography/F-L/Immelt-Jeffrey-R-1956.html

"General Electric Splits into 3 Companies." https://www.investopedia. com/general-electric-ge-splits-into-3-companies-5209130

"GE Plans to Form Three Public Companies Focused on Growth Sectors of Aviation, Healthcare, and Energy," press release, November 9, 2021. https://www.ge.com/news/press-releases/ ge-plans-to-form-three-public-companies-focused-on-growth-sectors-of-aviation

Market capitalization and revenue data on Tesla and General Motors are available on: https://finbox.com; https://companies marketcap.com, and https://www.google.com

"Visualizing the 25 Largest Private Equity Firms in the World." https://www.visualcapitalist.com/25-largest-private-equity-firms-chart/

"Elliott Takes Big Stake in Pernod, Maker of Absolut, Chivas Regal" – WSJ. https://www.wsj.com/articles/elliott-management-turns-its-attention-to-pernod-ricard-11544604974

CHAPTER 4

1. For an example of the SKUs portfolio of a Coca-Cola distributor, see https://www.cocacolaozarks.com/product/full-product-sku-list/

2. See, for instance, L.E.K. Consulting's report, "Ramping Up Revenue Management for CPG Firms." https://www.lek.com/insights/so/revenue-management-cpg

3. This example is based on a scenario of the REVMANEX simulator designed for training sales pros in value-capture. https://web.stratxsimulations.com/simulation/sales-and-negotiation-simulation

4. The customer satisfaction rating is not as readily measurable as profitability and market share. This will be addressed in Chapter 5.

5. You may find it strange that a positive profitability may destroy corporate value. Remember, however, that the costs used to estimate the profitability of a sales agreement are not the total costs. Each sales agreement therefore needs to produce a minimum profitability to pay for other fixed and indirect costs. In addition, the incentive formula should take into account an opportunity cost, i.e., the fact that the resources (e.g., products, supply chain, service, and so on) not used in an unattractive deal could be better deployed elsewhere.

CHAPTER 5

1. See, for instance, E.W. Anderson, C. Fornell, and D.R. Lehmann, "Customer Satisfaction, Market Share and Profitability: Findings from Sweden," *Journal of Marketing*, July (1994): 53–66, and

Matthew Young and Christine Ennew, "From Customer Satisfaction to Profitability," *Journal of Strategic Marketing*, online (2000): 313–326. For a specific study in the insurance sector, see David M. Pooser and Mark J. Browne, "The Effects of Customer Satisfaction on Company Profitability: Evidence from the Property and Casualty Insurance Industry," *Risk Management and Insurance Review*, September (2018).

2. David Bejou, Timothy Keiningham, and Lerzan Aksoy, *Customer Lifetime Value: Reshaping the Way We Manage to Maximize Profits* (New York: Routledge, 2006); V. Kumar, *Customer Lifetime Value: The Path to Profitability* (Boston: Now Publishers, 2008); Lloyd Melnick and Wendy Russ Beasley, *Understanding the Predictable: How to Calculate, Understand, and Improve Customer Lifetime Value to Build a Great Company* (Scotts Valley, CA: CreateSpace Independent Publishing Platform, 2015); The Art of Service, *Customer Lifetime Value: A Complete Guide* (Brendale, Queensland: Customer Lifetime Value Publishing, 2020).

3. In addition to the average CSAT score, other popular measures are the percentage CSAT score and the NPS (Net Promoter Score). See Terry G. Vavra, *Improving Your Measurement of Customer Satisfaction: A Guide to Creating, Conducting, Analyzing, and Reporting Customer Satisfaction Measurement Programs* (Milwaukee, WI: ASQ Quality Press, 1997); Douglas W. Hubbard, *How to Measure Anything: Finding the Value of Intangibles in Business* (3rd edition) (Hoboken, NJ: Wiley, 2014); Fred Reichheld, *The Ultimate Question 2.0: How Net Promoter Companies Thrive in a Customer-Driven World* (Boston: Harvard Business Review, 2011); Maurice FitzGerald, *Net Promoter - Implement the System: Advice and Experience from Leading Practitioners* (Zurich: SBVV, 2017).

4. See, for instance, Courtney E. Ackerman, "What Is Self-Expression? (20 Activities + Examples)," August 6, 2018. https://positivepsychology.com/self-expression/

5. Albert Mehrabian, *Silent Messages* (Marceline, MO: Wadsworth, 1971), p. 43.

FURTHER SOURCES

"Negotiation Research You Can Use: Recovering from Adverse Events in Negotiation," Program on Negotiation, Harvard Law School, December 31, 2018. https://www.pon.harvard.edu/daily/negotiation-skills-daily/negotiation-research-you-can-use-recovering-from-adverse-events-in-negotiation-nb/

"How Much Communication Is Really Nonverbal?," Premiere Global Services, blog by Sonya T., March 30, 2020. https://www.pgi.com/blog/2020/03/how-much-of-communication-is-really-nonverbal/

CHAPTER 6

1. James MacGregor Burns, *Leadership* (New York: HarperCollins, 1978), p. 2.

2. For some eminent books covering different facets of leadership, see John Maxwell, *The 21 Irrefutable Laws of Leadership: Follow Them and People Will Follow You* (London: Thomas Nelson, 1998); Dale Carnegie, *How to Win Friends & Influence People* (Mumbai: Sanage Publishing House, 2021) (the first edition was published by Simon & Schuster in 1936; this is one of the world's bestsellers and still current); Brené Brown, *Dare to Lead: Brave Work. Tough Conversations. Whole Heart* (New York:

Random House, 2018); Warren Bennis, *On Becoming a Leader* (New York: Basic Books, 1989); Manfred F.R. Kets de Vries, *The Leadership Mystique: A User's Manual for the Human Enterprise* (Englewood Cliffs, NJ: Prentice Hall, 2001); Peter G. Northouse, *Leadership: Theory and Practice* (Thousand Oaks, CA: SAGE, 2018); Jane E. Dutton and Gretchen M. Spreitzer, *How to Be a Positive Leader: Small Actions, Big Impact* (New York: Berrett-Koehler, 2018).

3. John Maxwell, *The 21 Irrefutable Laws of Leadership: Follow Them and People Will Follow You* (25th anniversary edition) (New York: HarperCollins, 2022).

4. See Howard Gardner, *Frames of Mind: The Theory of Multiple Intelligences* (New York: Basic Books, 1983).

5. Peter Salovey and John D. Mayer, "Emotional Intelligence," *Imagination, Cognition, and Personality*, 9 (1990): 185–211.

6. Daniel Goleman, *Emotional Intelligence* (New York: Bantam Books, 1995).

7. Aristotle also used a third concept "ethos," the influence exercised on others by the credibility of the speaker, which we will not develop here, but which corresponds to what we have called the "hard" side of leadership.

8. Stephen R. Covey, *The 7 Habits of Highly Effective People: Powerful Lessons in Personal Change* (25th anniversary edition) (New York: Simon & Schuster, 2013), p. 299.

9. Out of the myriad of books on leadership and personal development, I would particularly recommend: Marshall Goldsmith, *What Got You Here Won't Get You There: How Successful People Become Even More Successful* (London: Profile Books, 2013).

10. See Ryan Holiday, *Ego Is the Enemy* (London: Profile Books, 2017).

11. See, for instance, the tools developed by my colleague Professor Manfred Kets de Vries and available through KDVI at The Kets de Vries Institute. https://www.kdvi.com/tools

12. See, for instance, Linn Martinsen, *Therapy Toolkit: Sixty Cards for Self-Exploration* (London: Laurence King Publishing, 2021).

FURTHER SOURCES

"The Stanford-Binet Scale." https://dictionary.apa.org/stanford-binet-intelligence-scale

"What Is Business Acumen?," Acumen Learning, Business Acumen Training. https://www.acumenlearning.com/what-is-business-acumen

"Ego Is the Enemy of Good Leadership," by Louis Carter. https://louiscarter.com/ego-is-the-enemy-of-good-leadership/

"How Knowing Yourself Equals Better Leadership," by Ben Brearley. https://www.thoughtfulleader.com/knowing-yourself-better-leadership

CHAPTER 7

1. Chapters 1–6 correspond to this first module of the WAWS Programme, while Chapters 7–10 contain the elements of the second module focusing on negotiations and value capture.

2. Ronald M. Shapiro, *Dare to Prepare: How to Win Before You Begin!* (reprint edition) (New York; Currency, 2009), p. 21.

3. Sun Tzu, *The Art of War*, translated by Ralph D. Sawyer (New York: Basic Books, 1994).

4. Even in a zero-sum game, there should be no loser, but one party will win more than the other. The point is that the total to be shared is fixed.

5. For a list of the main variables in sales negotiations, see the Six Primary Variables excerpted from *The Negotiation Book: Your Definitive Guide to Successful Negotiating* by Steve Gates (Hoboken, NJ: Wiley, 2011). https://www.oreilly.com/library/view/the-negotiation-book/9780470664919/9780470664919_the_six_primary_variables.html

6. Note that commercial guidelines specify the variables, discount structure, and what the sales pro is allowed to do, as indicated earlier. Here, these are objectives on drivers, not to be confused with the guidelines.

7. Roger Fisher and William Ury, *Getting to Yes: Negotiating Agreement Without Giving In* (Boston: Houghton Mifflin, 1981).

8. The possibility of a negotiation on volume as well as price creates a BATNA frontier as opposed to just a BATNA value. This expands the range of options that can be considered by the seller.

FURTHER SOURCES

"The True Value of Negotiation Preparation." https://www.negotiate.org/the-true-value-of-negotiation-preparation/

"A Negotiation Preparation Checklist," PON, Program on Negotiation at Harvard Law School. https://www.pon.harvard.edu/daily/negotiation-skills-daily/negotiation-preparation-checklist/

"A Lot of You Have Asked about the Walmart Cheer." https://www.tiktok.com/@rickymunozjr/video/7111322776199318827?lang=en

CHAPTER 8

1. This is an expression often attributed to Benjamin Franklin. There is no published evidence he originated the saying and it is probably an aphorism that already existed before his time!

2. Many business writers confuse strategy and planning. The most fundamental reference in the field of strategy is still the oldest: *The Art of War*, by Sun Tzu, translated by Ralph D. Sawyer (New York: Basic Books, 1994), written in the fifth century BC. It is deep, concise and entertaining. For important contributions to the field of business strategy, see Richard Rumelt, *Good Strategy/Bad Strategy: The Difference and Why It Matters* (New York: Profile Books, 2017); Max McKeown, *The Strategy Book: How to Think and Act Strategically to Deliver Outstanding Results* (London: FT Press, 2019); and Avinash K. Dixit and Barry J. Nalebuff, *The Art of Strategy: A Game Theorist's Guide to Success in Business and Life* (New York: W.W. Norton, 2010).

3. The ZOPA concept is widely attributed to Roger Fisher and William Ury. In their bestseller *Getting to Yes: Negotiating Agreement Without Giving In* (Boston: Houghton Mifflin, 1981), there is, however, no explicit reference to ZOPA, contrary to their repeated use of BATNA. Only on page 137 is there a mention of a "zone of potential agreement." It seems that the acronym ZOPA was coined later through application of the BATNA concept.

4. See Chapter 5.

5. For an excellent and more complete account of possible failures in negotiations, see Chris Voss, *Never Split the Difference: Negotiating As If Your Life Depended on It* (New York: Harper Business, 2016).

6. The possibility of a negotiation on volume as well as price creates a BATNA frontier for the buyer as well as for the seller. This expands the range of negotiation possibilities relative to a fixed volume negotiation.

7. Note that the possibility of negotiating on volume as well as price creates a ZOPA area rather than a ZOPA range when price is the only consideration. The ZOPA space allows both buyer and seller the possibility of exploring a wider scope of potential agreements.

CHAPTER 9

1. Sir Francis Bacon (1561–1626), "Of Negotiating," in *Essays*, first published in 1597. https://bacon.thefreelibrary.com/The-Essays/47-1

2. See, for instance, Gregory Northcraft and Margaret Neale, "Experts, Amateurs, and Real Estate: An Anchoring-and-Adjustment Perspective on Property Pricing Decisions." *Organizational Behavior and Human Decision Processes*, 39 (1987); Adam Galinsky and Thomas Mussweiler, "First Offers as Anchors: The Role of Perspective-Taking and Negotiator Focus." *Journal of Personality and Social Psychology*, 81 (2001); Max H. Bazerman and Margaret A. Neal, *Negotiating Rationally* (New York: Free Press, 1994).

3. Carl Rogers and Richard Farson, *Active Listening* (Chicago, IL: Industrial Relations Center of the University of Chicago, 1957); see also Center for Creative Leadership, *Active Listening: Improve Your Ability to Listen and Lead* (Hoboken, NJ: Wiley, 2019); Nixaly Leonardo, *Active Listening Techniques: 30 Practical*

Tools to Hone Your Communication Skills (New York: Rockridge Press, 2020).

4. Albert Mehrabian, *Nonverbal Communication* (New York: Routledge, 2007); Albert Mehrabian, *Silent Messages: Implicit Communication of Emotions and Attitudes* (Marceline, MO: Wadsworth, 1972).

5. Joe Navarro, *The Dictionary of Body Language: A Field Guide to Human Behavior* (New York: William Morrow Paperbacks, 2018).

6. Albert Mehrabian, *Nonverbal Communication*.

CHAPTER 10

1. Paul Allen, *Idea Man: A Memoir by the Cofounder of Microsoft* (Harmondsworth: Penguin, 2012),

2. You can see Blake's "Always be closing" speech in the 1992 *Glengarry Glen Ross* movie at https://youtu.be/Q4PE2hSqVnk

3. The concept of "frontier" is novel in sales negotiations because of the volume variable. Most books on negotiations just talk about a single BATNA. Later in this chapter, we converge back to BATNA (and not frontier) when there is an agreement on volume and the only variable left to agree on is price.

FURTHER SOURCE

"The History of Microsoft." https://learn.microsoft.com/en-us/shows/history/history-of-microsoft-1991

CHAPTER 11

1. Michael M. Lombardo and Robert W. Eichinger, *The Career Architect Development Planner* (1st edition) (Minneapolis, MN: Lominger, 1996). See also the 4th edition (Minneapolis, MN: Lominger, 2004). https://www.ccl.org/articles/leading-effectively-articles/70-20-10-rule/

2. See, for instance, Miles Hewstone, *Attribution Theory: Social and Functional Extensions*, (Oxford: Blackwell, 1983); Seymour L. Zelen, *New Models, New Extensions of Attribution Theory: The Third Attribution-Personality Theory Conference* (Berlin: Springer, 1988); Mark J. Martinko, *Attribution Theory in the Organizational Sciences: Theoretical and Empirical Contributions* (Charlotte, NC: Information Age, 2006).

3. John C. Maxwell, *Sometimes You Win—Sometimes You Learn: Life's Greatest Lessons Are Gained from Our Losses* (New York: Center Street, 2015).

4. Jean Cocteau (1889–1963) was a French novelist and multi-talented artist, poet, playwright, designer, and filmmaker.

5. In order, these quotations are from Seneca, Roman philosopher; Louis Pasteur, French chemist and microbiologist; Benjamin Franklin, American Founding Father and scientist; Thomas Jefferson, American Founding Father, third President of the United States; and Gary Player, South African golf champion.

6. For an excellent piece on the role of luck in selling, see Joël Le Bon, "Why the Best Salespeople Get So Lucky," *Harvard Business Review*, April 13, 2015.

FURTHER SOURCES

"Cutty Sark Greenwich." https://twitter.com/cuttysark/status/
    449139492960862209

"Where It All Began—A Race Around the Isle of Wight,"
    America's Cup. https://www.americascup.com/history/1_
    WHERE-IT-ALL-BEGAN-A-RACE-AROUND-THE-
    ISLE-OF-WIGHT

"The Origin of the Term 'Devil's Advocate' Is More Literal Than
    You Think," All That's Interesting, January 2, 2018. https://
    allthatsinteresting.com/devils-advocate-origin

See the Sales and Negotiation Simulation REVMANEX by StratX
    Simulations at https://web.stratxsimulations.com/simulation/
    sales-and-negotiation-simulation

INDEX